GRAPHIC MODERN HISTORY: WORLD WAR II

BATTLE FOR THE ATLANTIC

By Gary Jeffrey & Illustrated by Terry Riley

 Crabtree Publishing Company
www.crabtreebooks.com

Crabtree Publishing Company
www.crabtreebooks.com

Created and produced by:
  David West Children's Books
Project development, design, and concept:
  David West Children's Books
Author and designer: Gary Jeffrey
Illustrator: Terry Riley
Editor: Lynn Peppas
Proofreader: Wendy Scavuzzo

Project coordinator: Kathy Middleton
Production and print coordinator:
  Katherine Berti
Prepress technician: Katherine Berti
Photographs:
  Bundesarchiv: pages 4t, 4b, 5b, 6t,
  46 Simon Quinton: page 6b U.S.
  Navy: page 7b

Library and Archives Canada Cataloguing in Publication

CIP available at Library and Archives Canada

Library of Congress Cataloging-in-Publication Data

Jeffrey, Gary.
Battle for the Atlantic / Gary Jeffrey ; illustrated by Terry Riley.
p. cm. -- (Graphic modern history. World War II)
Includes index.
ISBN 978-0-7787-4192-3 (reinforced library binding : alk.
paper) -- ISBN 978-0-7787-4199-2 (pbk. : alk. paper) -- ISBN
978-1-4271-7872-5 (electronic pdf) -- ISBN 978-1-4271-7987-6
(electronic html)
1. World War, 1939-1945--Campaigns--Atlantic Ocean--Comic
books, strips, etc. 2. World War, 1939-1945--Campaigns--
Atlantic Ocean--Juvenile literature. 3. Graphic novels. I. Riley,
Terry. II. Title.

D770.J39 2012
940.54'293--dc23
                              2011050086

Crabtree Publishing Company
www.crabtreebooks.com   1-800-387-7650

Printed in Canada/012012/MA20111130

Published in Canada
Crabtree Publishing
616 Welland Ave.
St. Catharines, Ontario
L2M 5V6

Published in the United States
Crabtree Publishing
PMB 59051
350 Fifth Avenue, 59th Floor
New York, New York 10118

Published in the United Kingdom
Crabtree Publishing
Maritime House
Basin Road North, Hove
BN41 1WR

Published in Australia
Crabtree Publishing
3 Charles Street
Coburg North
VIC 3058

CONTENTS

SEA WARS

The declaration of war by Britain and France against Germany was barely nine hours old on Sunday, September 3, 1939, when two torpedoes sped towards Canada-bound British ship SS *Athenia*. An explosion ripped through the hull, stopping the engines, and she slowly began to sink. The Battle of the Atlantic had begun.

Oberleutnant Fritz-Julius Lemp had the dubious honor of sinking the first British ship of World War II.

OPENING SALVOES

The attack on *Athenia* by the German submarine U-30 had been a mistake. The U-boat's commander, Fritz-Julius Lemp, had incorrectly identified the passenger liner as an armed merchant ship (fair game under international prize rules) and had fired without warning. The death toll was 118. To Britain, this seeming act of unrestricted submarine warfare was an outrage.

In fact, U-30 was one of only 17 U-boats at sea from a fleet of just 27 suitable for Atlantic service in 1939. The British and French surface fleets outnumbered the Kriegsmarine (German navy) ten to one, but the ships that Germany had were formidable.

On September 12, the First Lord of the Admiralty, Winston Churchill, declared an armed convoy system would begin ferrying supplies to Britain from allies and friendly neutral countries such as the United States.

While German battleships headed to the Atlantic to begin raiding, U-boats managed to sink a Royal Navy aircraft carrier and a battleship at anchor, as well as 114 merchant ships. As 1939 drew to a close, even with nine U-boats sunk, the outlook for the Allies did not look promising.

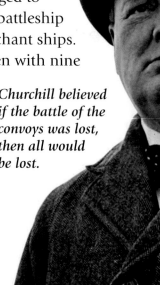

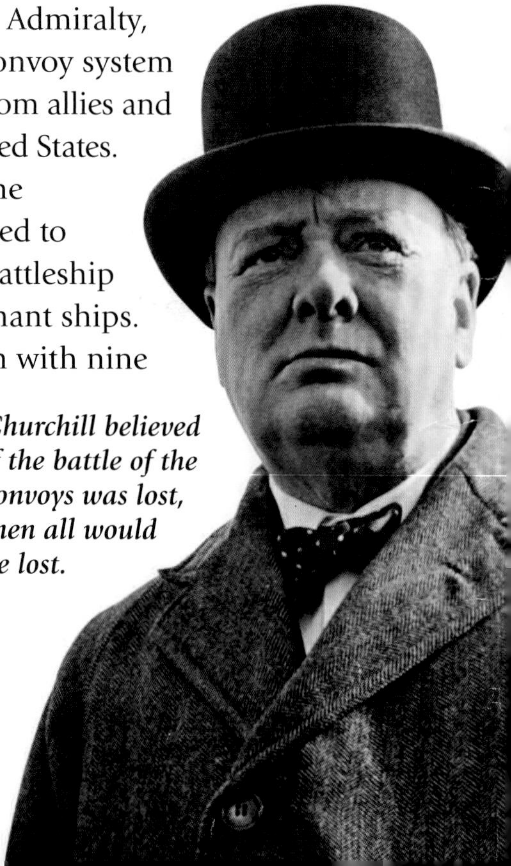

Churchill believed if the battle of the convoys was lost, then all would be lost.

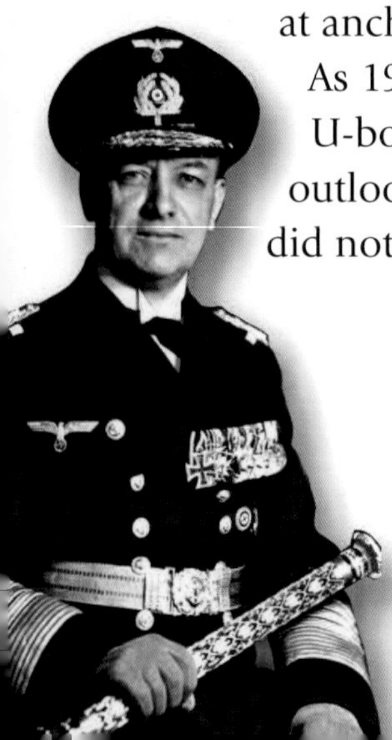

Kriegsmarine Grand Admiral Erich Raeder was counting on Germany's warships to sink the bulk of the Atlantic convoys.

Battle of the River Plate

The pocket battleship *Admiral Graf Spee* had been prowling the waters of the South Atlantic since the war began, operating a successful hit-and-run campaign against unarmed merchant ships. Her captain Hans Langsdorff was honoring prize rules and evacuating the ships' crews before sending the cargo carriers down.

On December 13, 1939, a squadron of three British cruisers intercepted the *Admiral Graf Spee*. After a 30-minute running battle, with one British warship severely damaged and another partially disabled, the battle-scarred *Admiral Graf Spee* made for Montevideo Harbor on the River Plate, Uruguay.

Langsdorff had a dilemma. Damage to his fuel filters meant he would be unable to reach Germany. The British fooled him into thinking they had a great number of ships waiting outside the harbor. Langsdorff scuttled his ship and committed suicide.

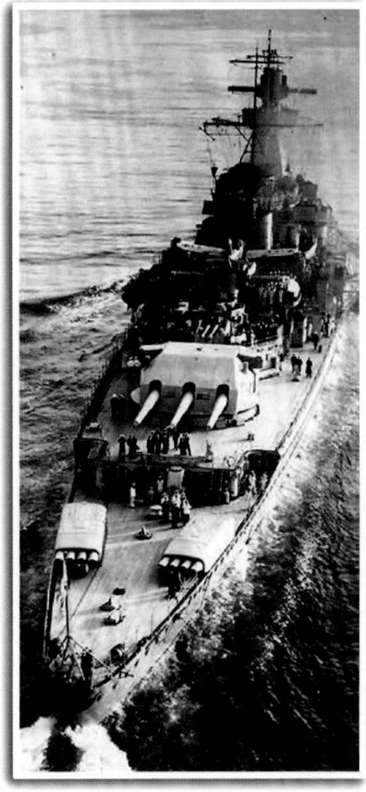

Germany's Deutschland class cruisers such as **Admiral Graf Spee** *were so heavily armed the Allies called them "pocket battleships."*

Sea Wolves

After the fall of France in June 1940, U-boat bases were rapidly constructed along the western French coast. The North Atlantic convoys would now be within easy reach of the more than 20 new U-boats a month being built in Germany. The initiative was driven by Commander of Submarines, Karl Dönitz. A veteran of submarine warfare in World War I, Dönitz believed the improved Type VII U-boats and their dedicated crews should be allowed to hunt in groups, but his grand strategy would have to wait until enough U-boats came on line.

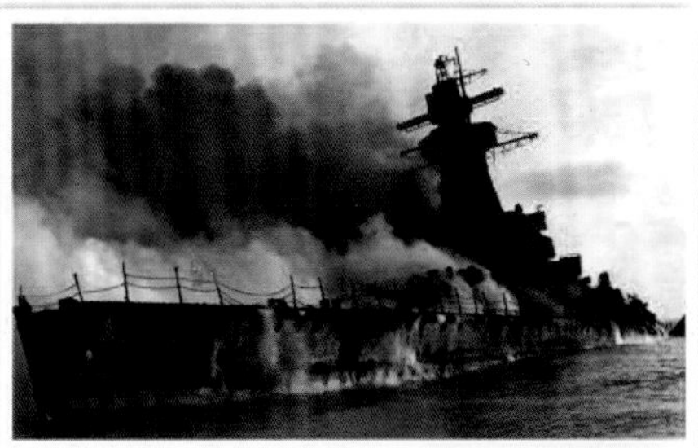

Admiral Graf Spee *ablaze and sinking on December 17, 1939—a loss Germany could ill afford.*

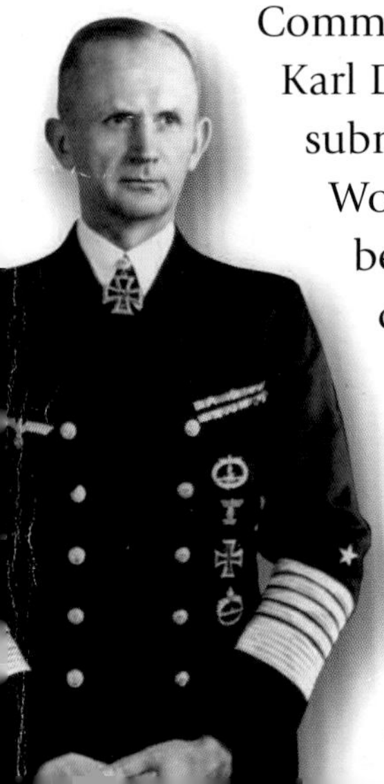

When invasion plans were shelved after the Battle of Britain, Rear Admiral Karl Dönitz thought commerce raiding by U-boat alone could starve Britain into surrendering.

HIGH-STAKES GAME

*Pride of the German fleet was the Bismarck class battleships of which there were two—*Bismarck *and* Tirpitz.

The year 1940 had ended with 567 Allied merchant ships sunk compared to only 24 U-boats. The U-boat commanders and their crews were hailed as heroes by the German public, while Churchill, now Britain's prime minister, privately worried that the "wolf packs" would destroy the convoys.

FIGHT BACK

The Germans had lost three of their most important ships during the invasion of Norway and, during raids in the Atlantic, were ordered to avoid contact with all British warships. So, when battleships *Scharnhorst* and *Gneisenau* went raiding between January and March 1941, they hit and ran, destroying or capturing 22 merchant ships with no loss to the Kriegsmarine.

HMS **Hood** *was the Royal Navy's premier battleship of World War II.*

Plans were made to put the mighty *Bismarck* to work using the same strategy.

Wolf pack operations didn't let up, and the Allies were cheered when top-scoring U-boat ace Günther Prien and U-47 disappeared while in action against British ships. Further victories against the aces commanding U-99 and U-100 came a few days later.

A German three-rotor Enigma encryption machine

On May 8, Fritz-Julius Lemp also found himself cornered by destroyers. After abandoning the crippled U-110, Lemp looked back and saw that the U-boat wasn't sinking as planned. He tried to swim back but was dragged under. The British successfully boarded the U-110 and recovered a vital Enigma machine and its paperwork.

While British codebreakers set to work breaking the German navy's code, the *Bismarck* and her heavy cruiser escort were steaming toward the Denmark Strait and an appointment with destiny.

United States Rides Point

During the second half of 1941, fortune seemed to swing in Britain's favor. More U-boats were patrolling than ever, yet far fewer merchant ships were being sunk. Following the loss of *Bismarck,* the Germans were reluctant to risk their surface fleet which was then bombed repeatedly by the RAF at port.

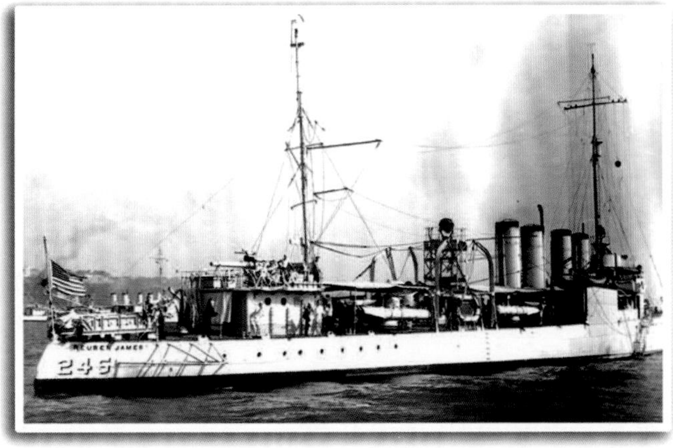

An old four-stack destroyer, the USS **Reuben James,** *became the first American warship lost in World War II when it was torpedoed on October 31, 1941.*

The constant reading of Kriegsmarine signal traffic had enabled convoys to be rerouted away from the wolf packs. The US Navy was also escorting convoys and mounting patrols as far east as Iceland in an unofficial war against the U-boats.

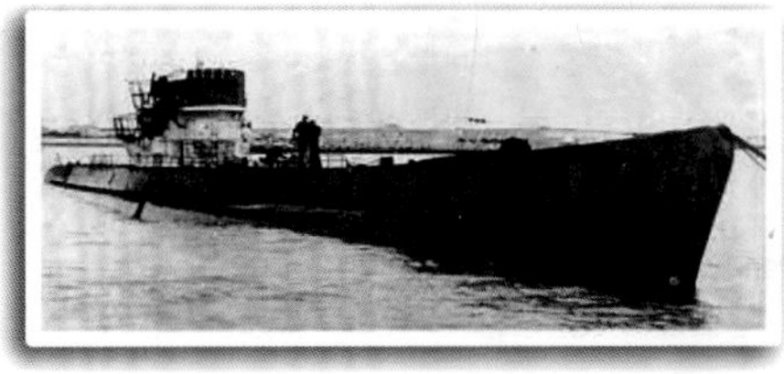

A Type IX U-boat

Operation Drumbeat

The conflict became official on December 11, 1941, when Germany, who had allied with Japan, declared war on the United States. Dönitz was delighted—here was a chance to attack US shipping industry and tip the balance in the Axis's favor. Dönitz christened it Operation Drumbeat—a drum roll before a performance, and a return to the "happy time" before the Allies had gained the upper hand. In January 1942, five larger Type IX U-boats set sail for the eastern seaboard to destroy the totally unprepared United States. There was no coastal blackout to hide ships, no convoy, and no anti-submarine escorts. To make matters worse, the Germans had added another rotor to their naval Enigmas, completely changing the code.

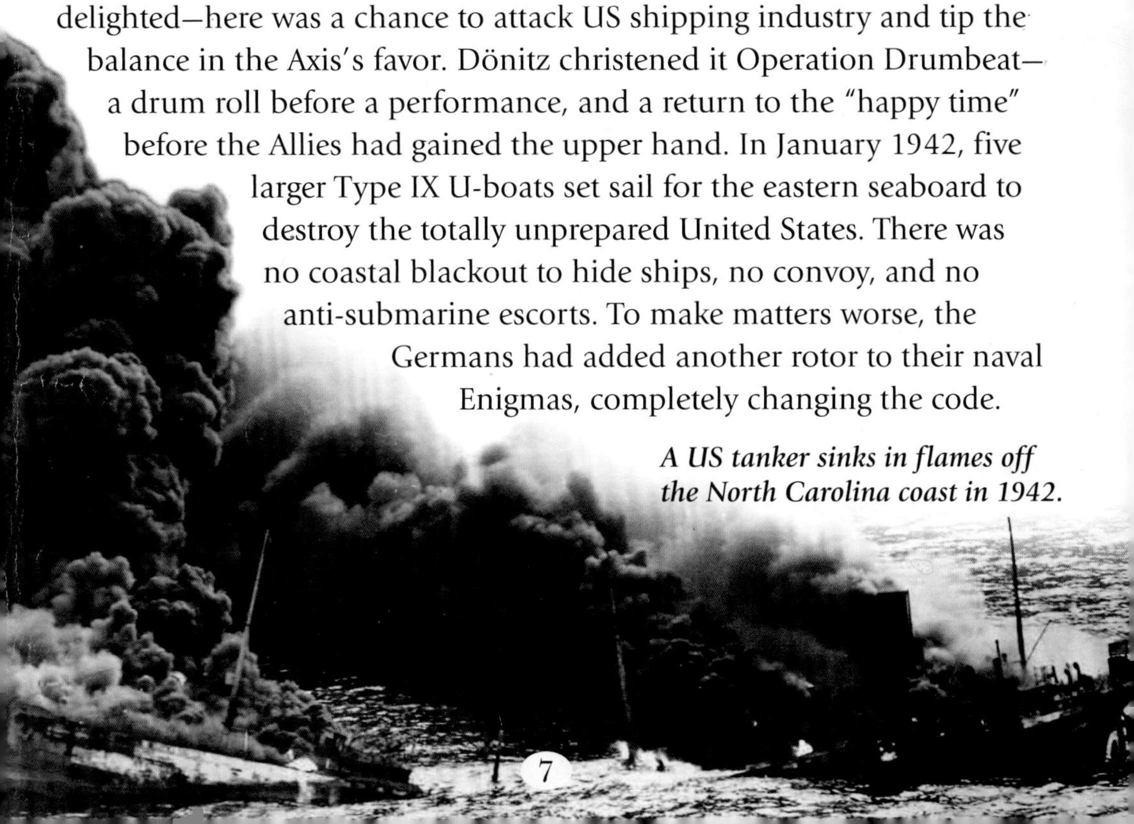

A US tanker sinks in flames off the North Carolina coast in 1942.

JOACHIM SCHEPKE AND OTTO KRETSCHMER
THE FATES OF U-100 AND U-99 —THE ATLANTIC WOLF PACK
MARCH 16, 1941

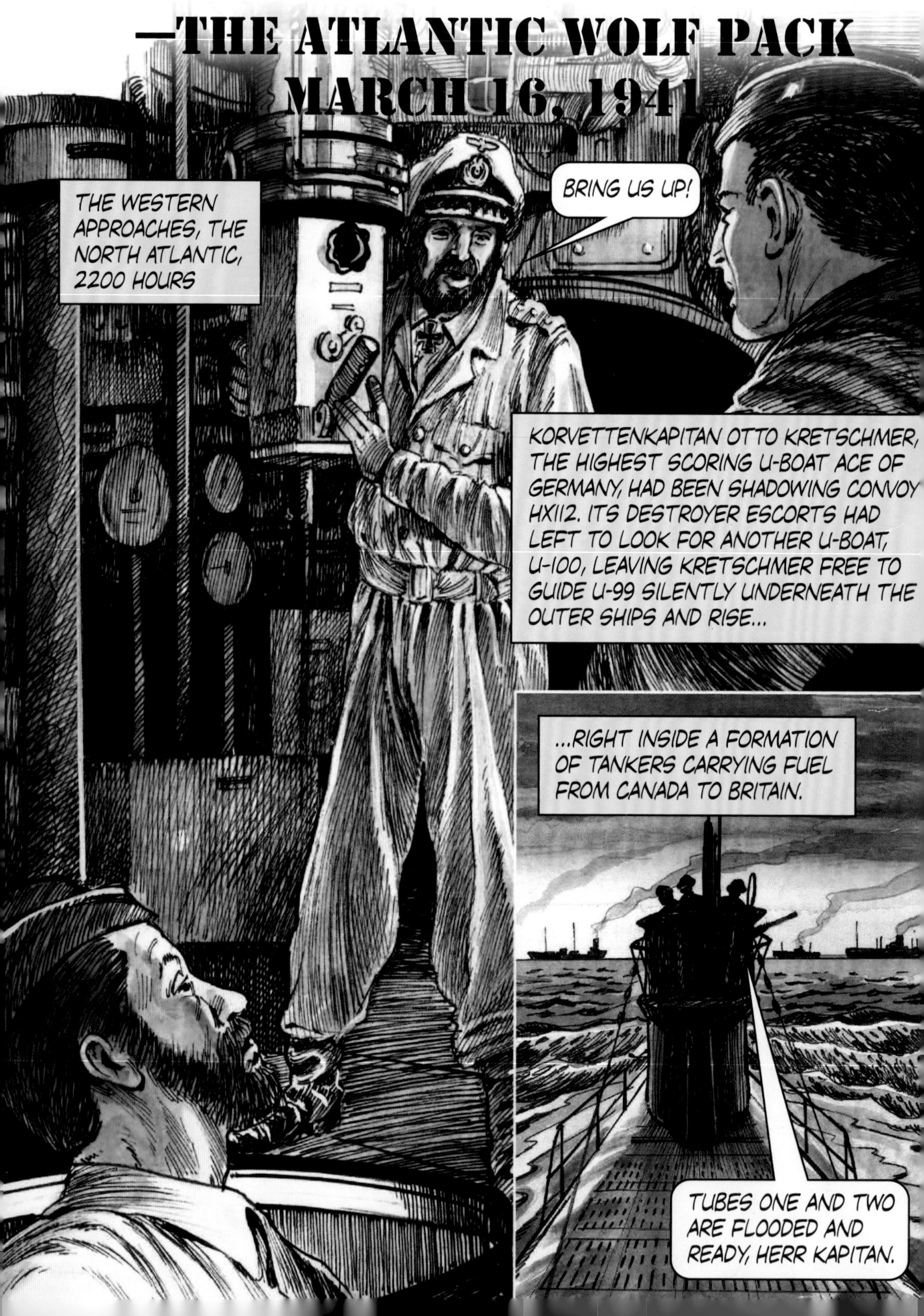

THE WESTERN APPROACHES, THE NORTH ATLANTIC, 2200 HOURS
BRING US UP!
KORVETTENKAPITAN OTTO KRETSCHMER, THE HIGHEST SCORING U-BOAT ACE OF GERMANY, HAD BEEN SHADOWING CONVOY HX112. ITS DESTROYER ESCORTS HAD LEFT TO LOOK FOR ANOTHER U-BOAT, U-100, LEAVING KRETSCHMER FREE TO GUIDE U-99 SILENTLY UNDERNEATH THE OUTER SHIPS AND RISE...
...RIGHT INSIDE A FORMATION OF TANKERS CARRYING FUEL FROM CANADA TO BRITAIN.
TUBES ONE AND TWO ARE FLOODED AND READY, HERR KAPITAN.

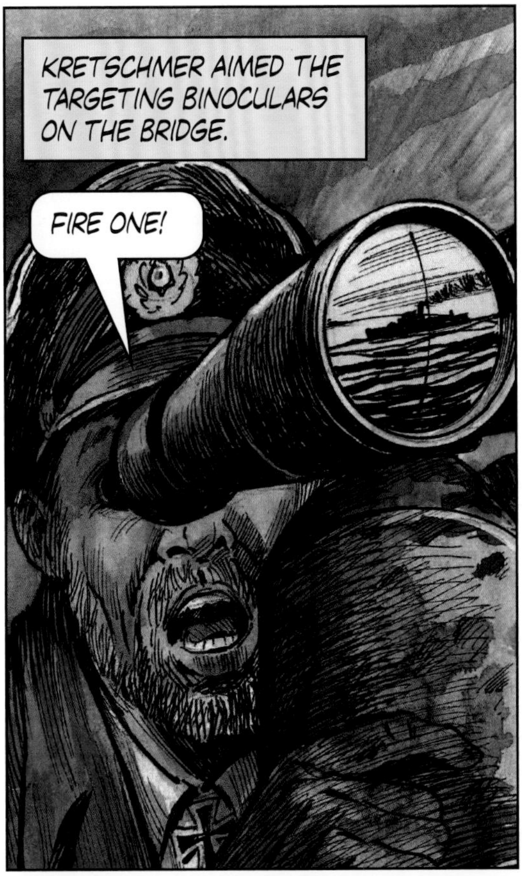
KRETSCHMER AIMED THE TARGETING BINOCULARS ON THE BRIDGE.
FIRE ONE!

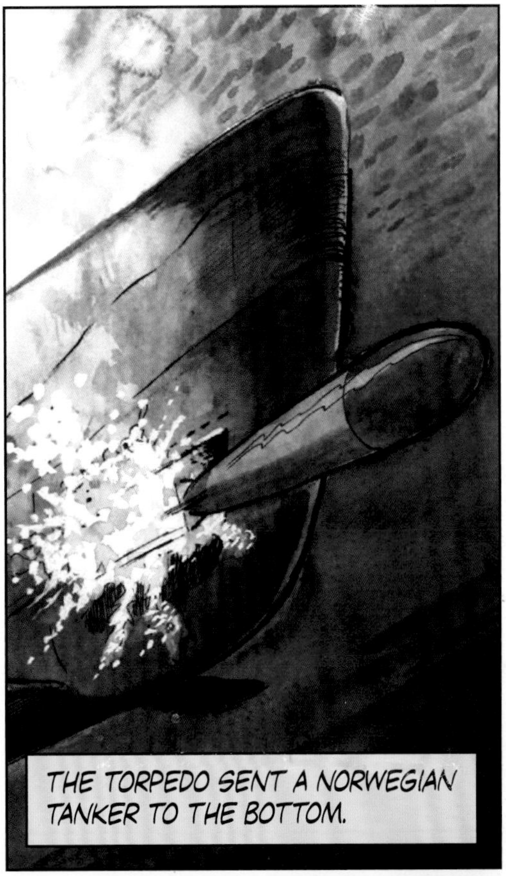
THE TORPEDO SENT A NORWEGIAN TANKER TO THE BOTTOM.

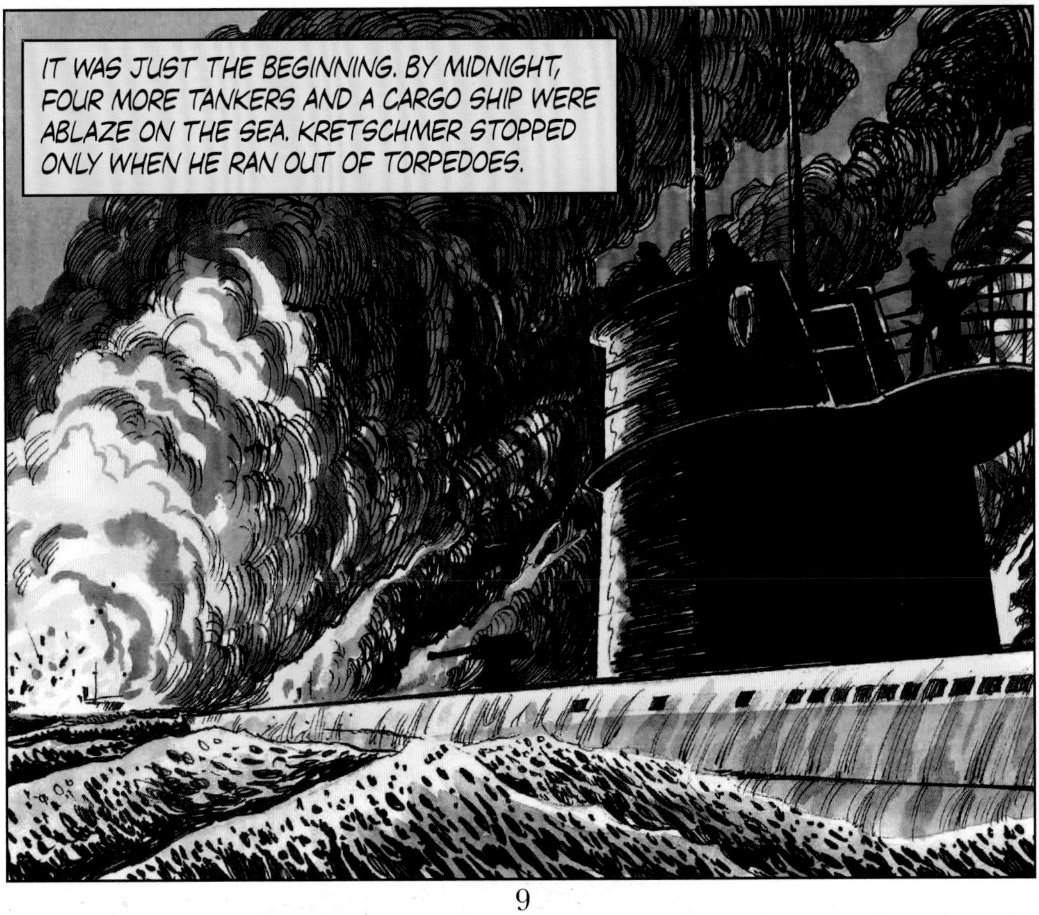
IT WAS JUST THE BEGINNING. BY MIDNIGHT, FOUR MORE TANKERS AND A CARGO SHIP WERE ABLAZE ON THE SEA. KRETSCHMER STOPPED ONLY WHEN HE RAN OUT OF TORPEDOES.

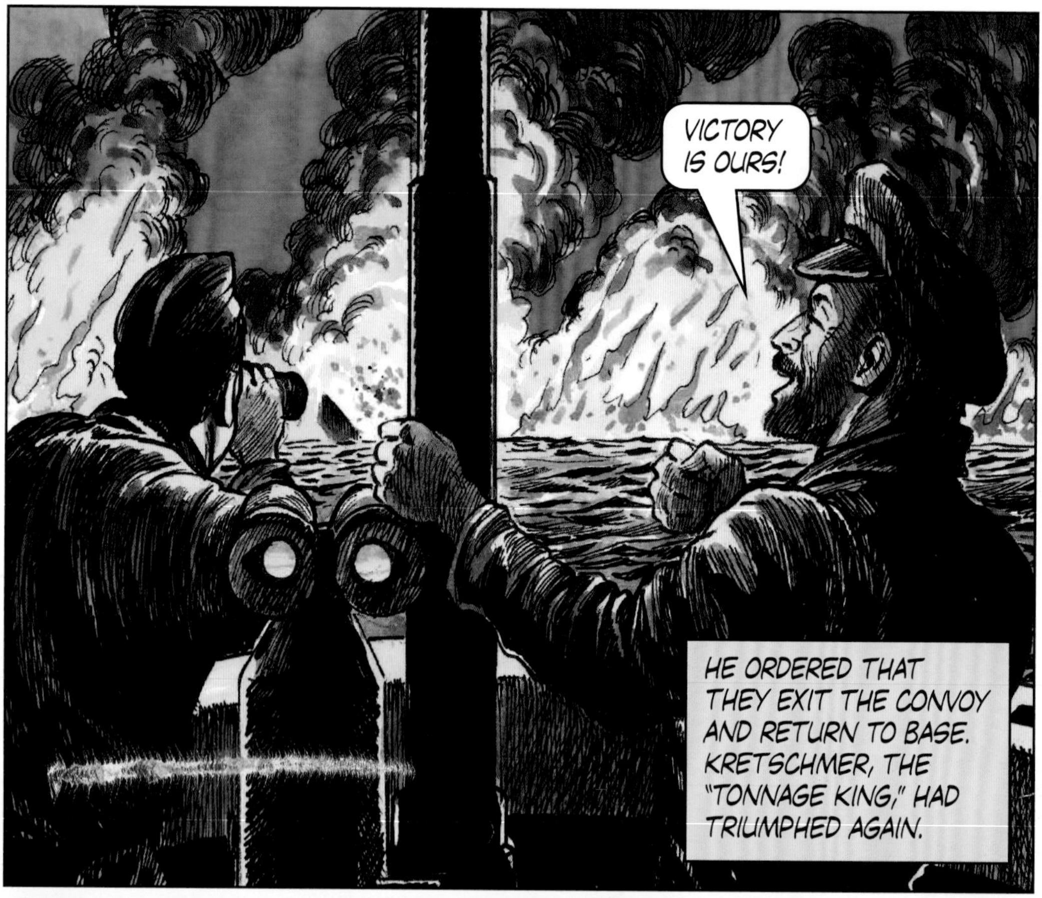
VICTORY IS OURS!
HE ORDERED THAT THEY EXIT THE CONVOY AND RETURN TO BASE. KRETSCHMER, THE "TONNAGE KING," HAD TRIUMPHED AGAIN.

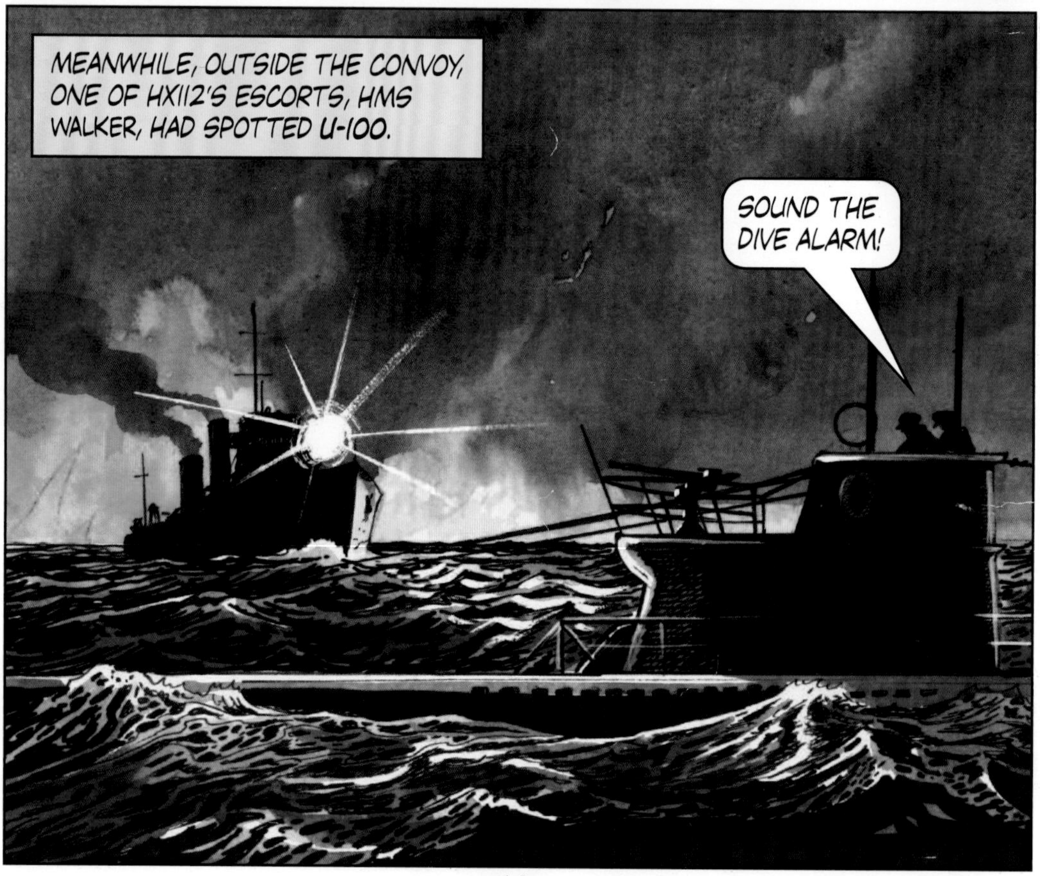
MEANWHILE, OUTSIDE THE CONVOY, ONE OF HX112'S ESCORTS, HMS WALKER, HAD SPOTTED U-100.
SOUND THE DIVE ALARM!

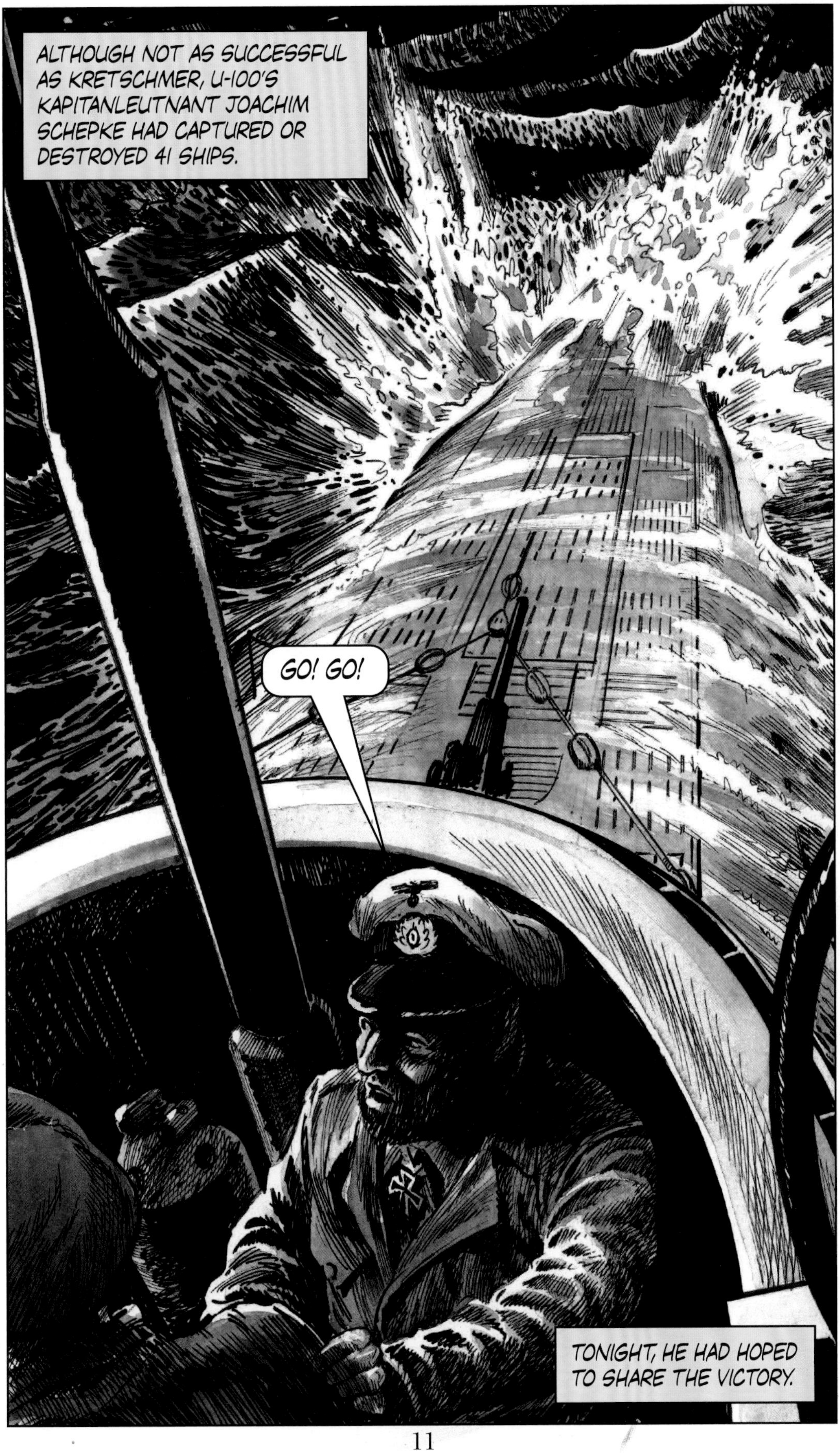
ALTHOUGH NOT AS SUCCESSFUL AS KRETSCHMER, U-100'S KAPITANLEUTNANT JOACHIM SCHEPKE HAD CAPTURED OR DESTROYED 41 SHIPS.
GO! GO!
TONIGHT, HE HAD HOPED TO SHARE THE VICTORY.

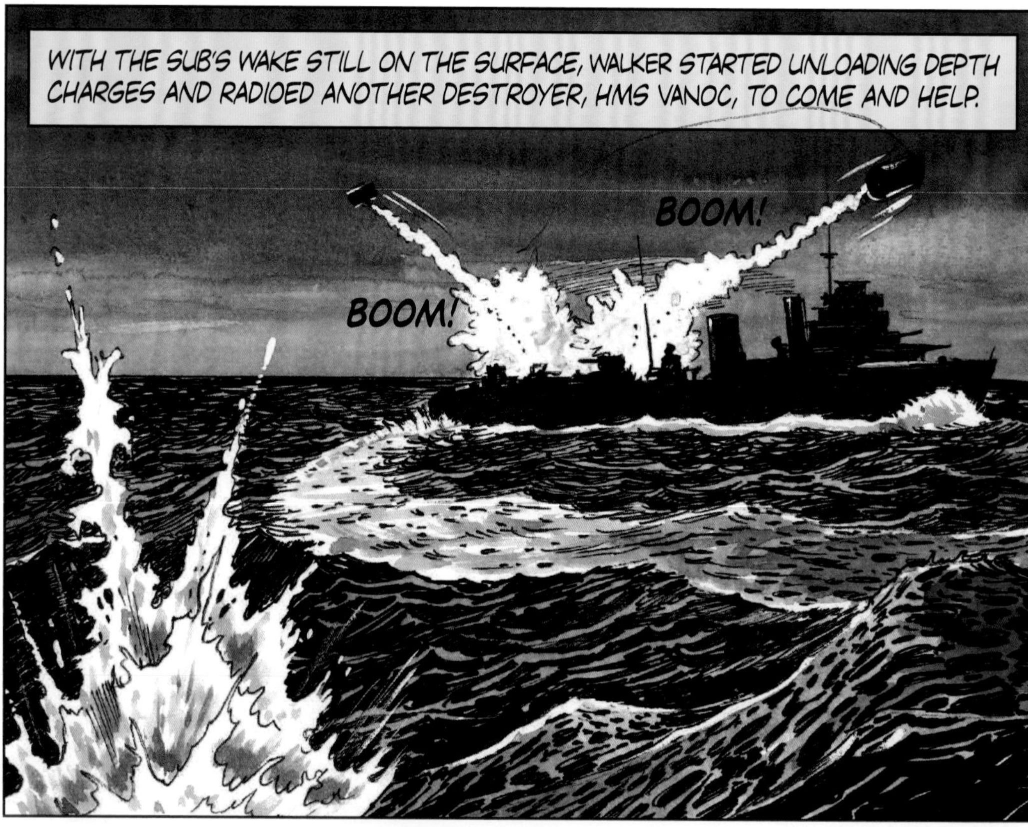
WITH THE SUB'S WAKE STILL ON THE SURFACE, WALKER STARTED UNLOADING DEPTH CHARGES AND RADIOED ANOTHER DESTROYER, HMS VANOC, TO COME AND HELP.
BOOM!
BOOM!

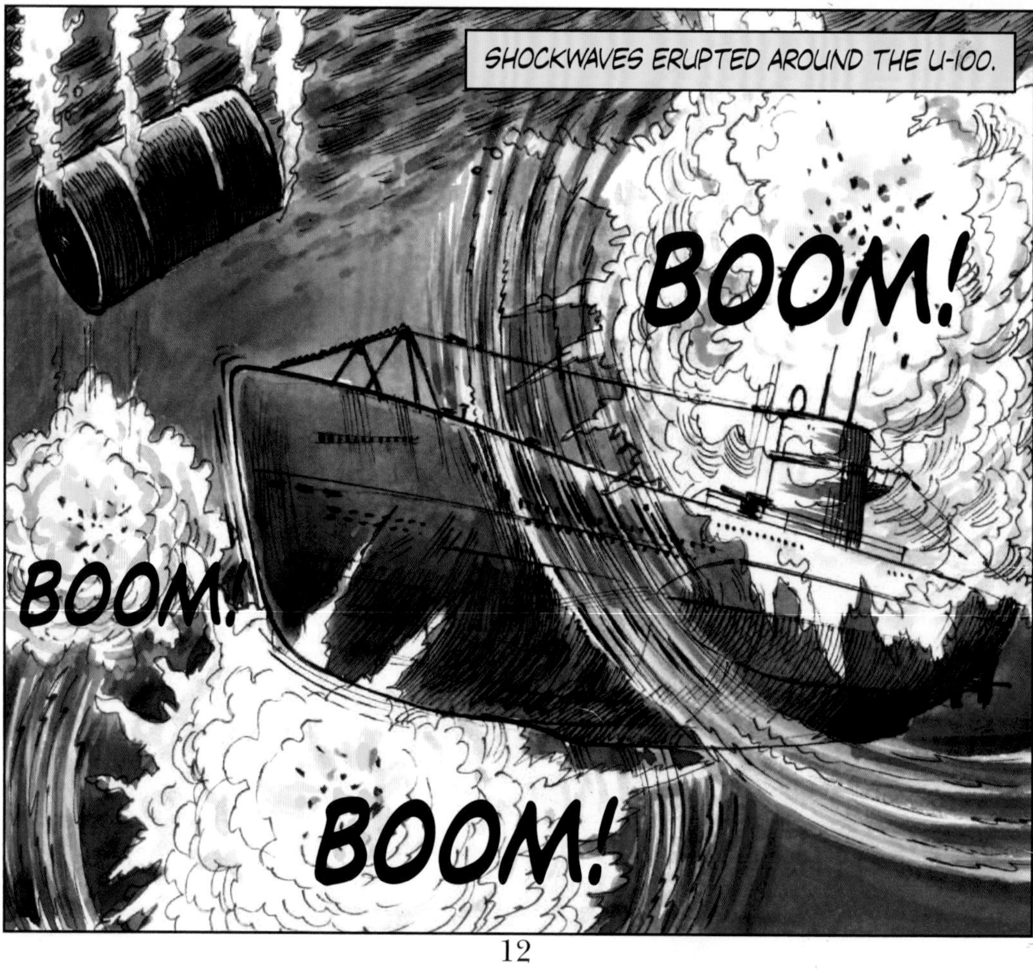
SHOCKWAVES ERUPTED AROUND THE U-100.
BOOM!
BOOM!
BOOM!

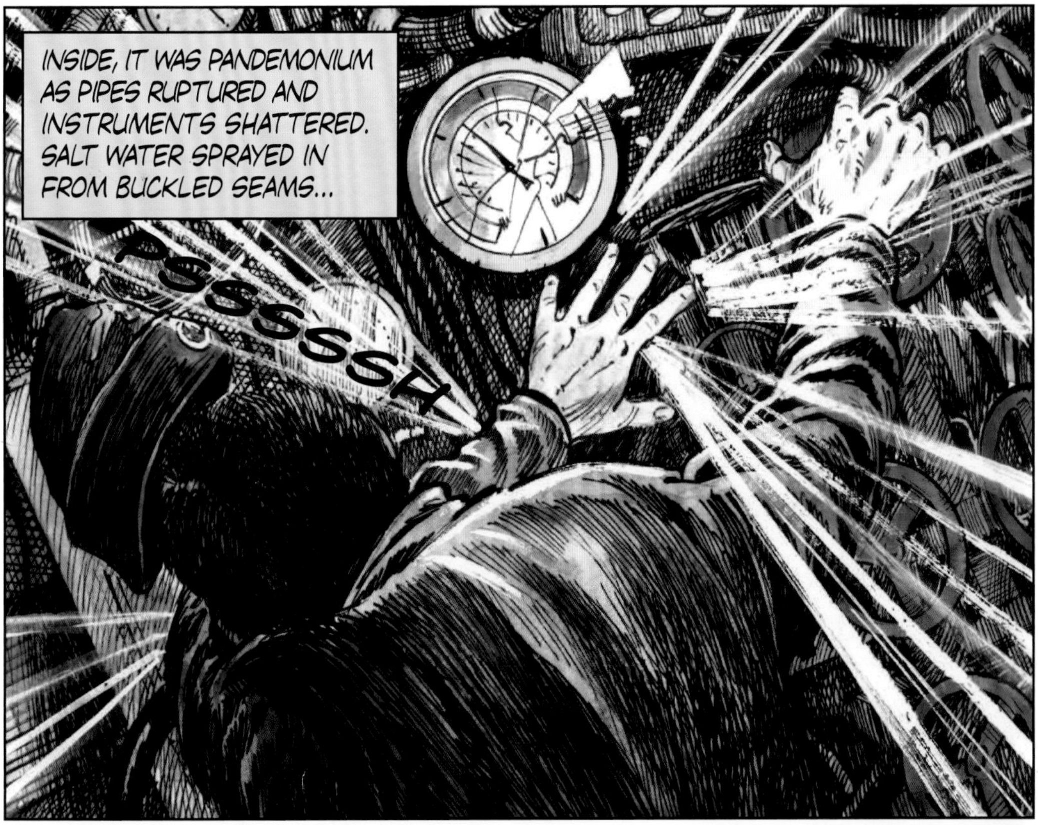
INSIDE, IT WAS PANDEMONIUM AS PIPES RUPTURED AND INSTRUMENTS SHATTERED. SALT WATER SPRAYED IN FROM BUCKLED SEAMS...
PSSSSSSH

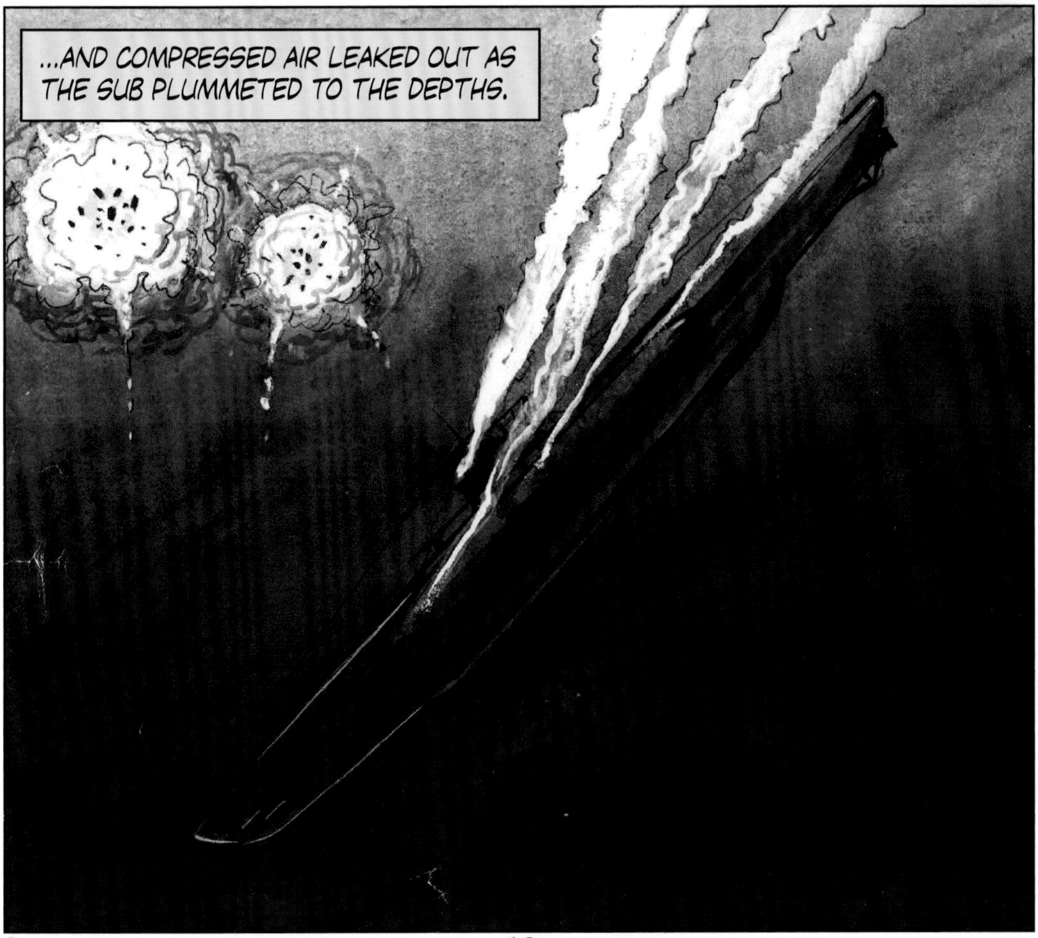
...AND COMPRESSED AIR LEAKED OUT AS THE SUB PLUMMETED TO THE DEPTHS.

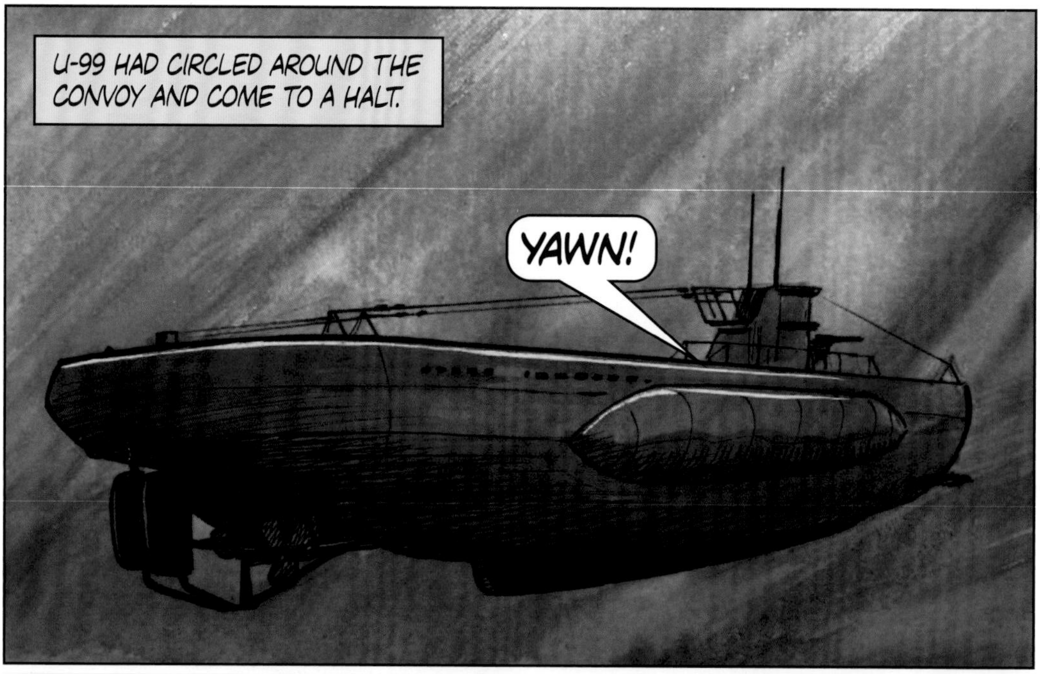
U-99 HAD CIRCLED AROUND THE CONVOY AND COME TO A HALT.
YAWN!

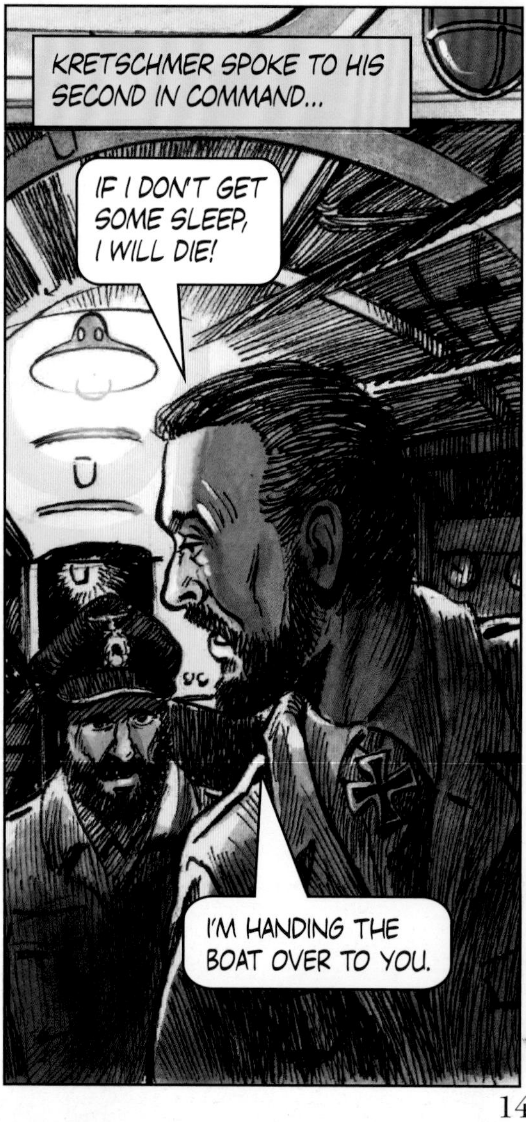
KRETSCHMER SPOKE TO HIS SECOND IN COMMAND...
IF I DON'T GET SOME SLEEP, I WILL DIE!
I'M HANDING THE BOAT OVER TO YOU.

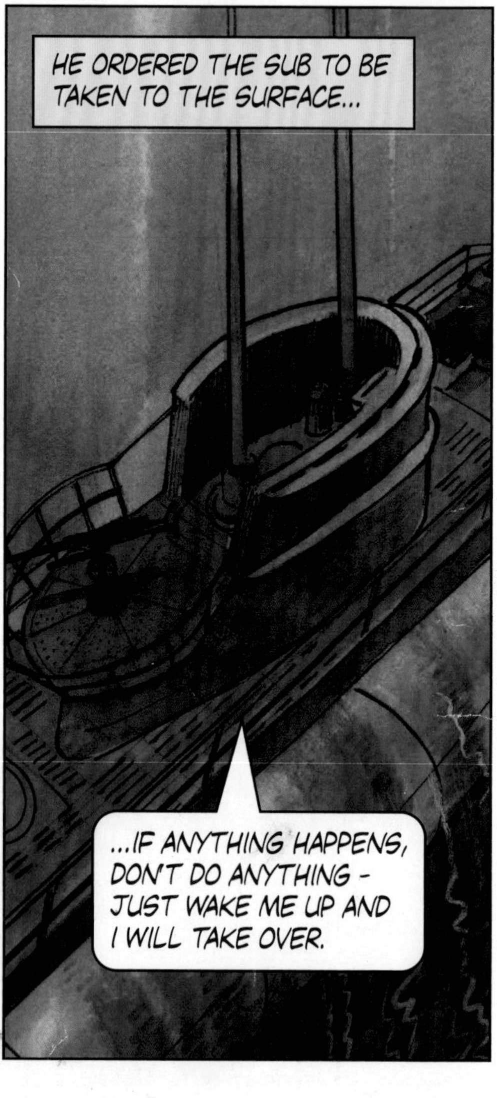
HE ORDERED THE SUB TO BE TAKEN TO THE SURFACE...
...IF ANYTHING HAPPENS, DON'T DO ANYTHING - JUST WAKE ME UP AND I WILL TAKE OVER.

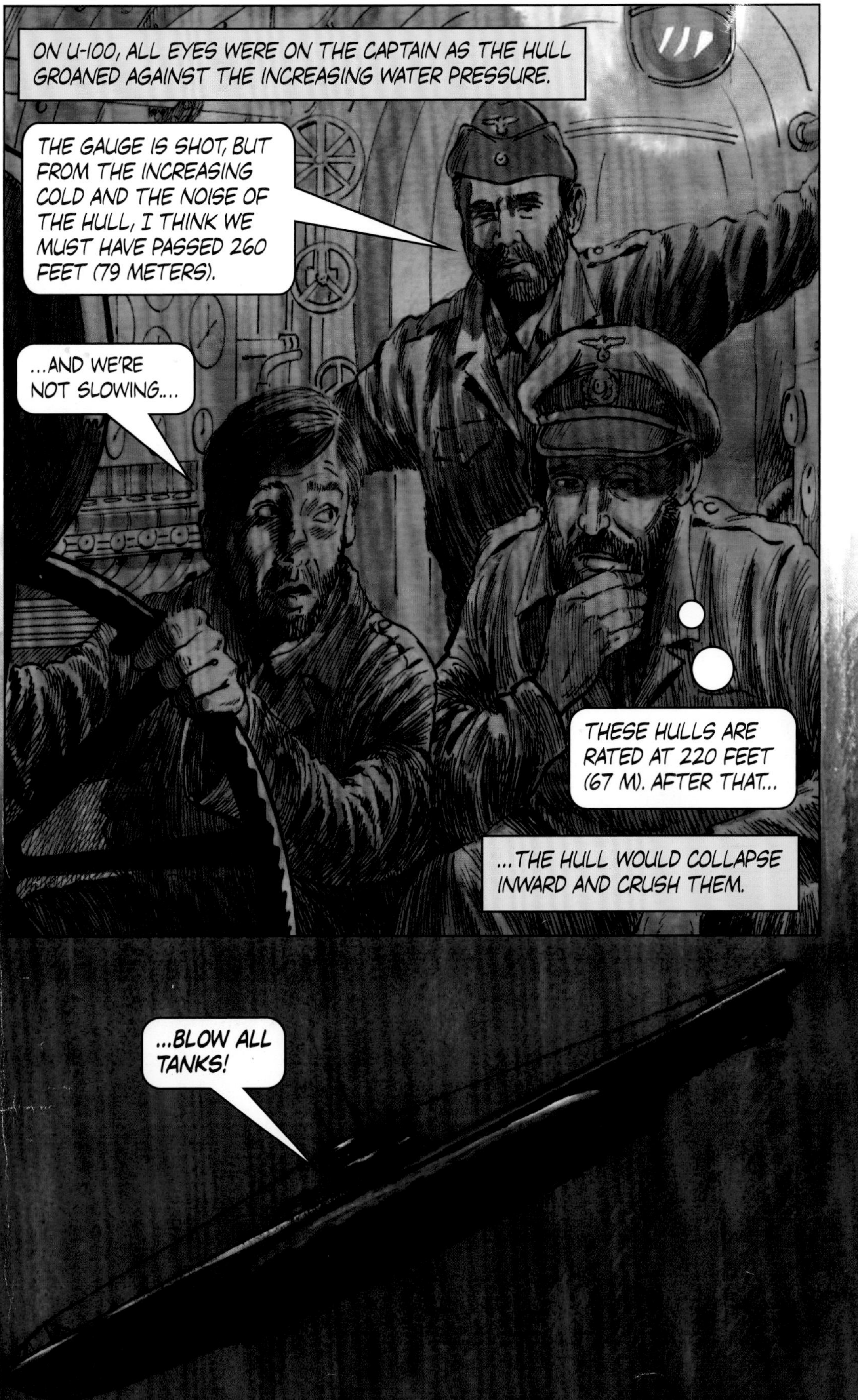
ON U-100, ALL EYES WERE ON THE CAPTAIN AS THE HULL GROANED AGAINST THE INCREASING WATER PRESSURE.
THE GAUGE IS SHOT, BUT FROM THE INCREASING COLD AND THE NOISE OF THE HULL, I THINK WE MUST HAVE PASSED 260 FEET (79 METERS).
...AND WE'RE NOT SLOWING....
THESE HULLS ARE RATED AT 220 FEET (67 M). AFTER THAT...
...THE HULL WOULD COLLAPSE INWARD AND CRUSH THEM.
...BLOW ALL TANKS!

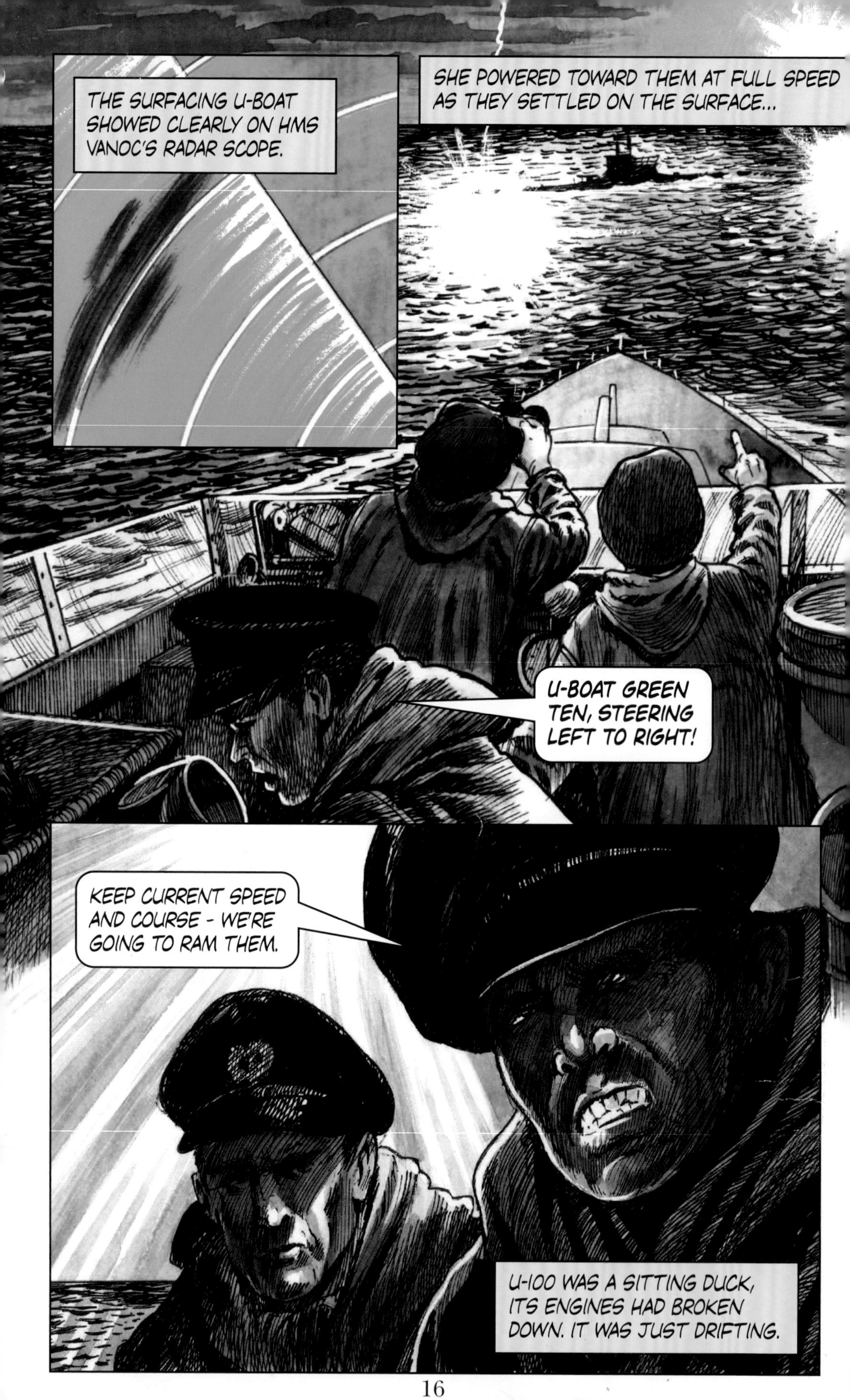
THE SURFACING U-BOAT SHOWED CLEARLY ON HMS VANOC'S RADAR SCOPE.
SHE POWERED TOWARD THEM AT FULL SPEED AS THEY SETTLED ON THE SURFACE...
U-BOAT GREEN TEN, STEERING LEFT TO RIGHT!
KEEP CURRENT SPEED AND COURSE - WE'RE GOING TO RAM THEM.
U-100 WAS A SITTING DUCK, ITS ENGINES HAD BROKEN DOWN. IT WAS JUST DRIFTING.

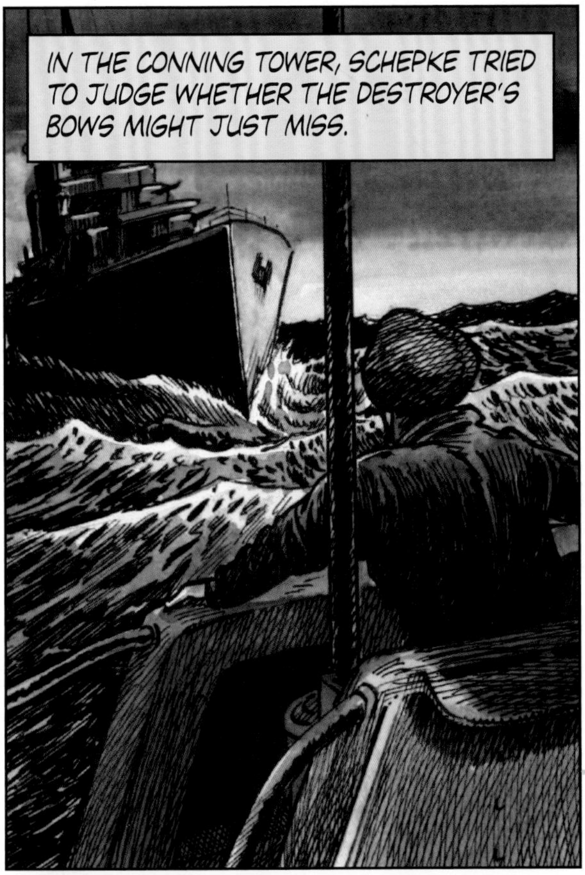
IN THE CONNING TOWER, SCHEPKE TRIED TO JUDGE WHETHER THE DESTROYER'S BOWS MIGHT JUST MISS.

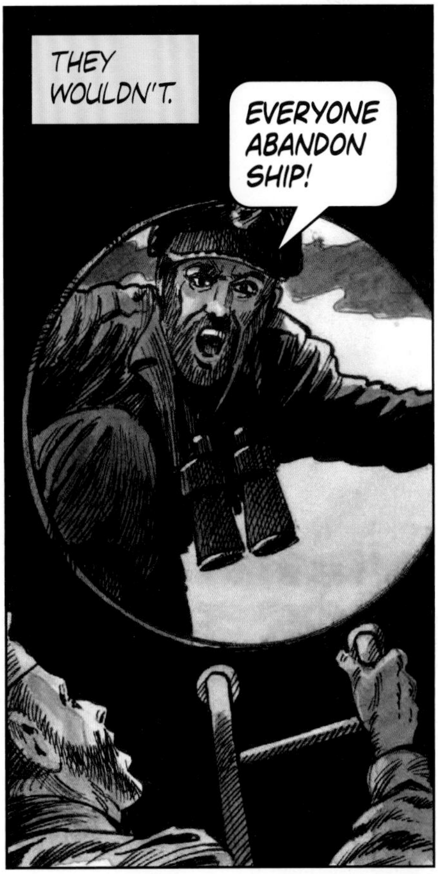
THEY WOULDN'T.
EVERYONE ABANDON SHIP!

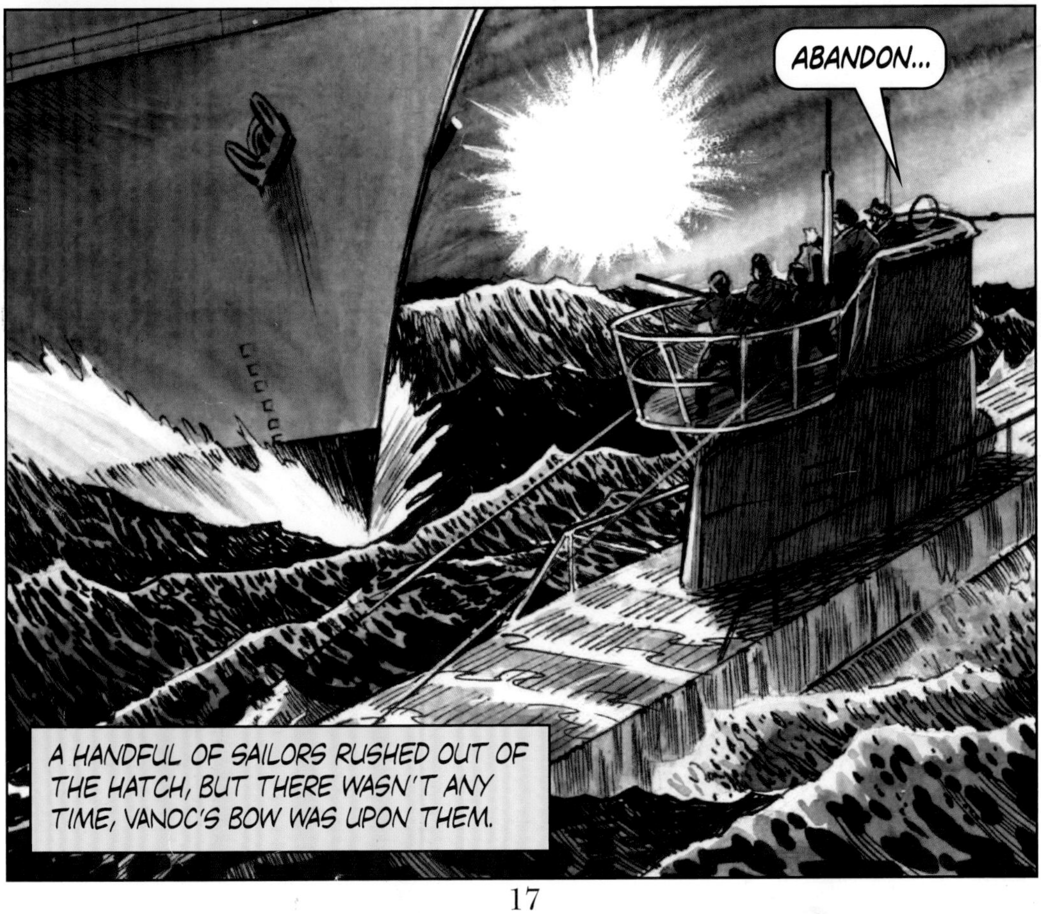
ABANDON...
A HANDFUL OF SAILORS RUSHED OUT OF THE HATCH, BUT THERE WASN'T ANY TIME, VANOC'S BOW WAS UPON THEM.

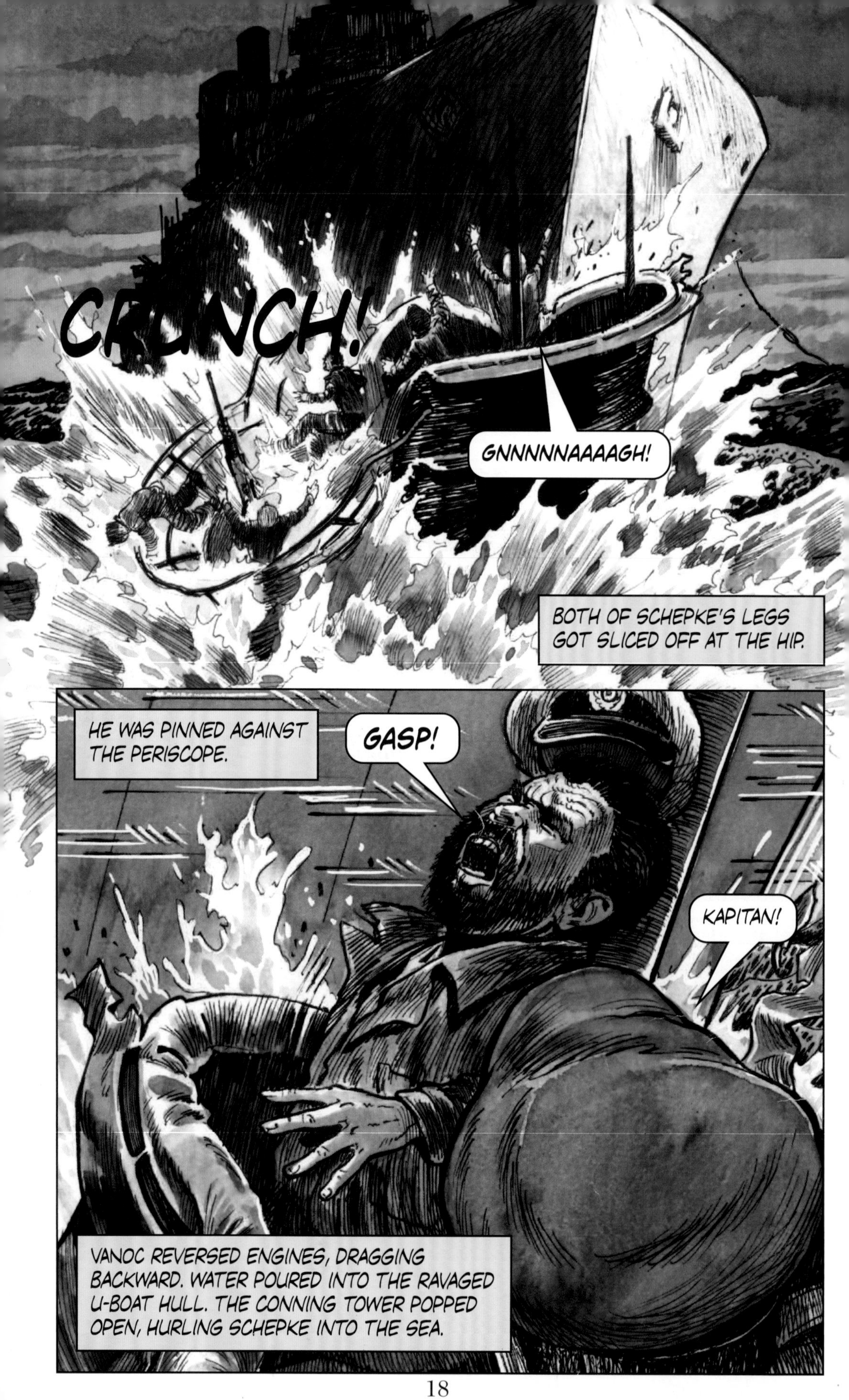
CRUNCH!
GNNNNNAAAAGH!
BOTH OF SCHEPKE'S LEGS GOT SLICED OFF AT THE HIP.
HE WAS PINNED AGAINST THE PERISCOPE.
GASP!
KAPITAN!
VANOC REVERSED ENGINES, DRAGGING BACKWARD. WATER POURED INTO THE RAVAGED U-BOAT HULL. THE CONNING TOWER POPPED OPEN, HURLING SCHEPKE INTO THE SEA.

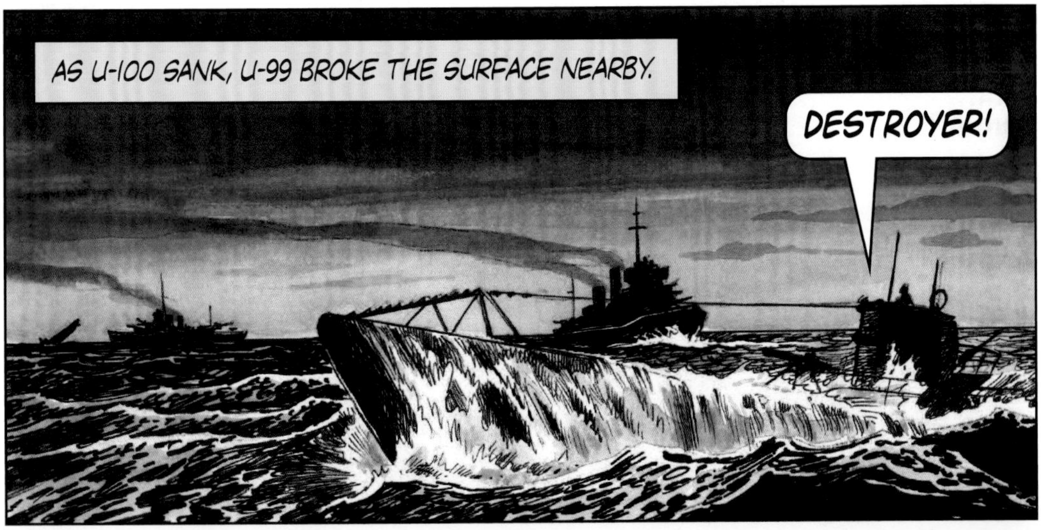
AS U-100 SANK, U-99 BROKE THE SURFACE NEARBY.
DESTROYER!

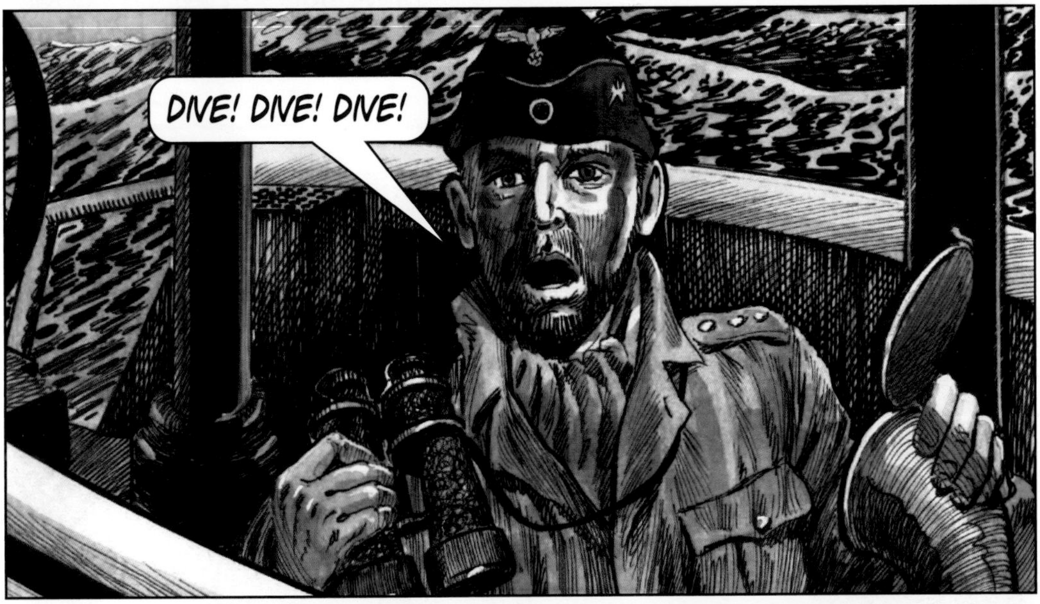
DIVE! DIVE! DIVE!

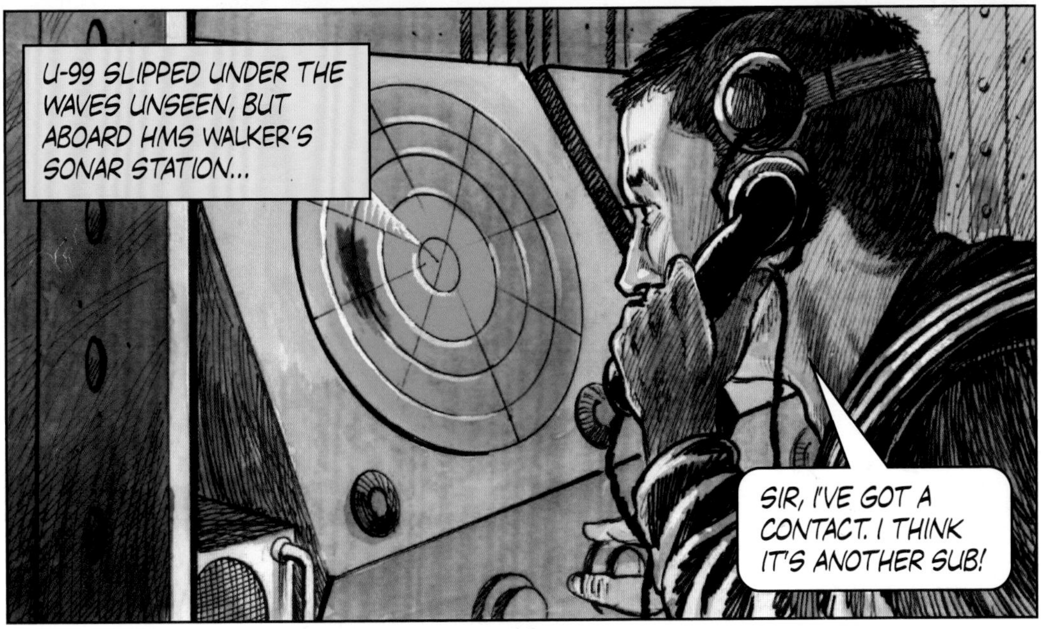
U-99 SLIPPED UNDER THE WAVES UNSEEN, BUT ABOARD HMS WALKER'S SONAR STATION...
SIR, I'VE GOT A CONTACT. I THINK IT'S ANOTHER SUB!

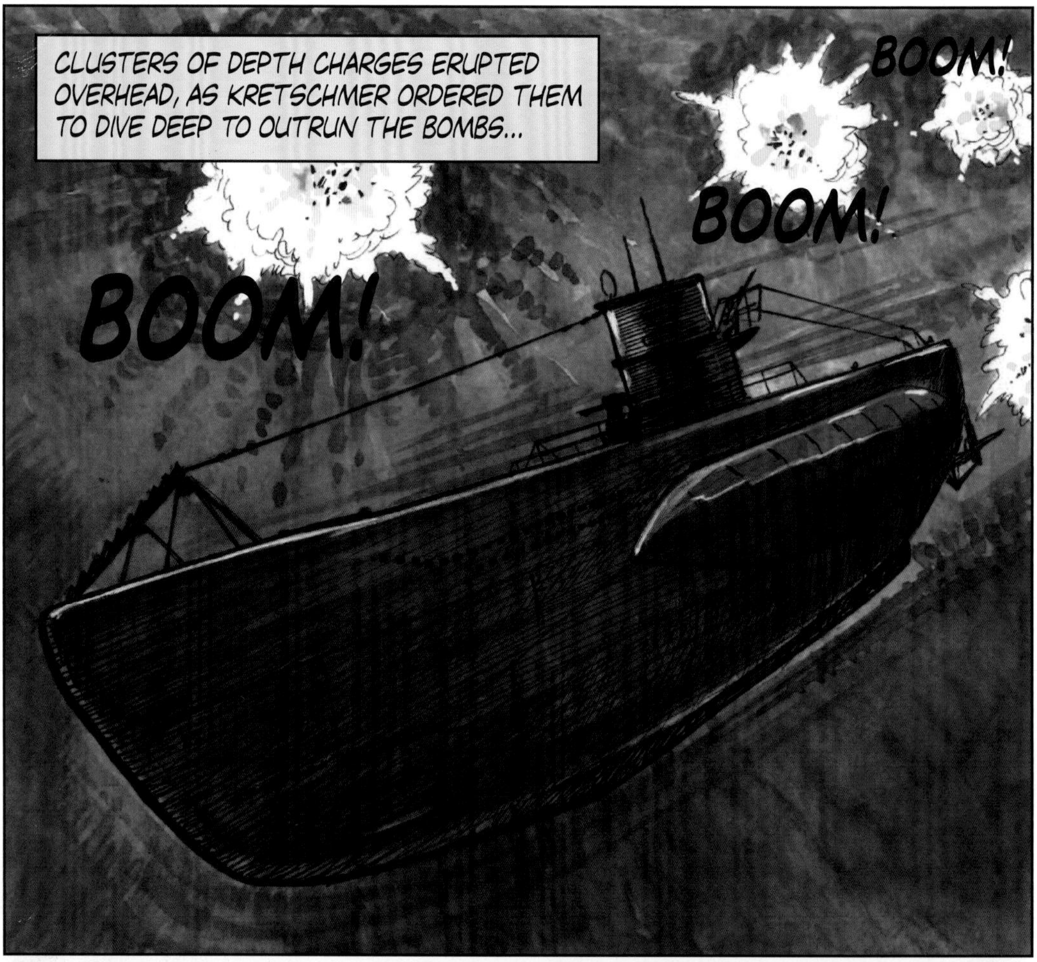
CLUSTERS OF DEPTH CHARGES ERUPTED OVERHEAD, AS KRETSCHMER ORDERED THEM TO DIVE DEEP TO OUTRUN THE BOMBS...
BOOM!
BOOM!
BOOM!

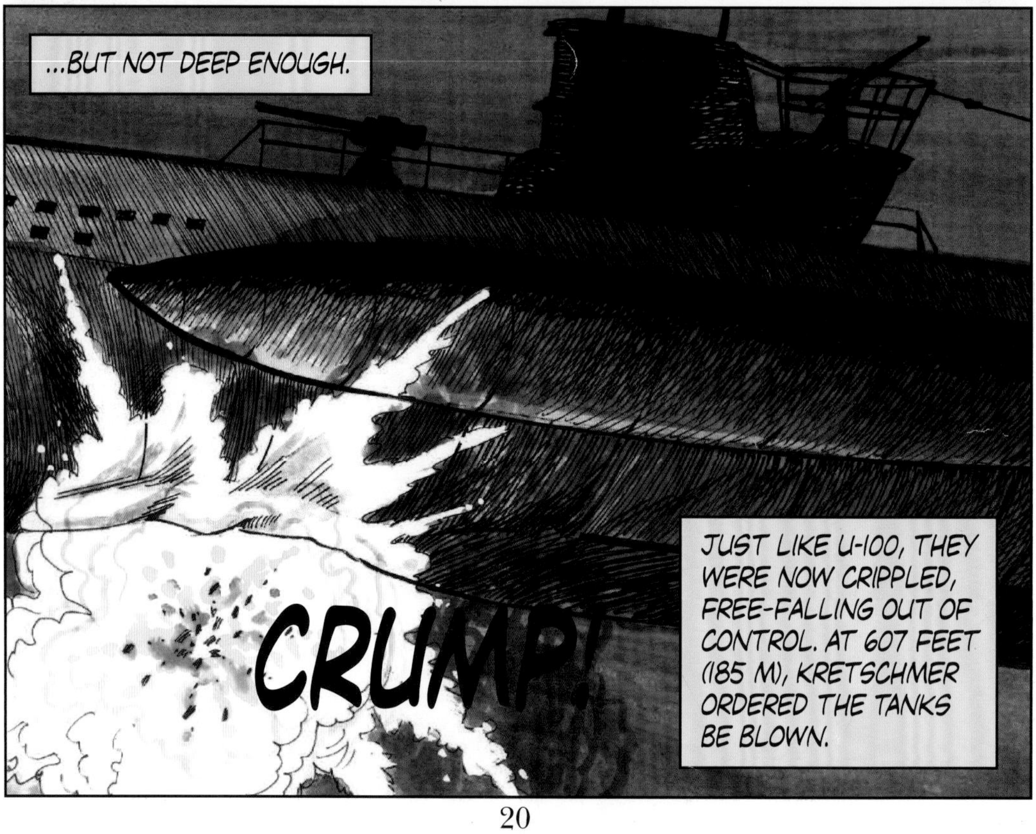
...BUT NOT DEEP ENOUGH.
CRUMP!
JUST LIKE U-100, THEY WERE NOW CRIPPLED, FREE-FALLING OUT OF CONTROL. AT 607 FEET (185 M), KRETSCHMER ORDERED THE TANKS BE BLOWN.

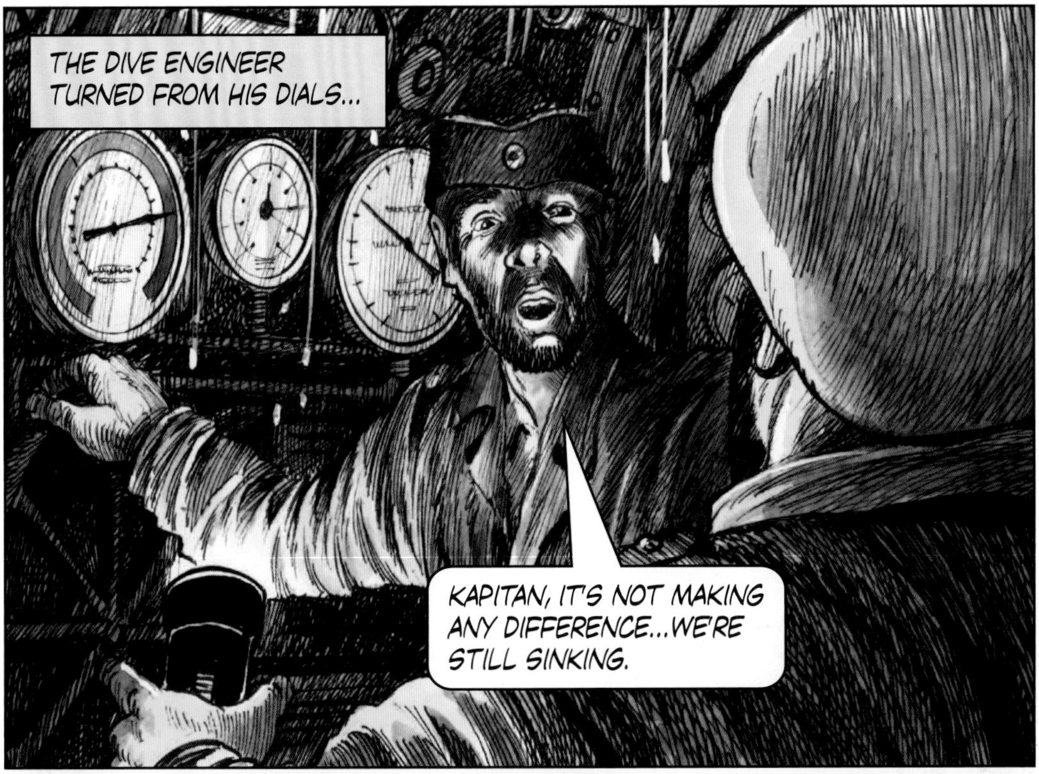
THE DIVE ENGINEER TURNED FROM HIS DIALS...
KAPITAN, IT'S NOT MAKING ANY DIFFERENCE...WE'RE STILL SINKING.

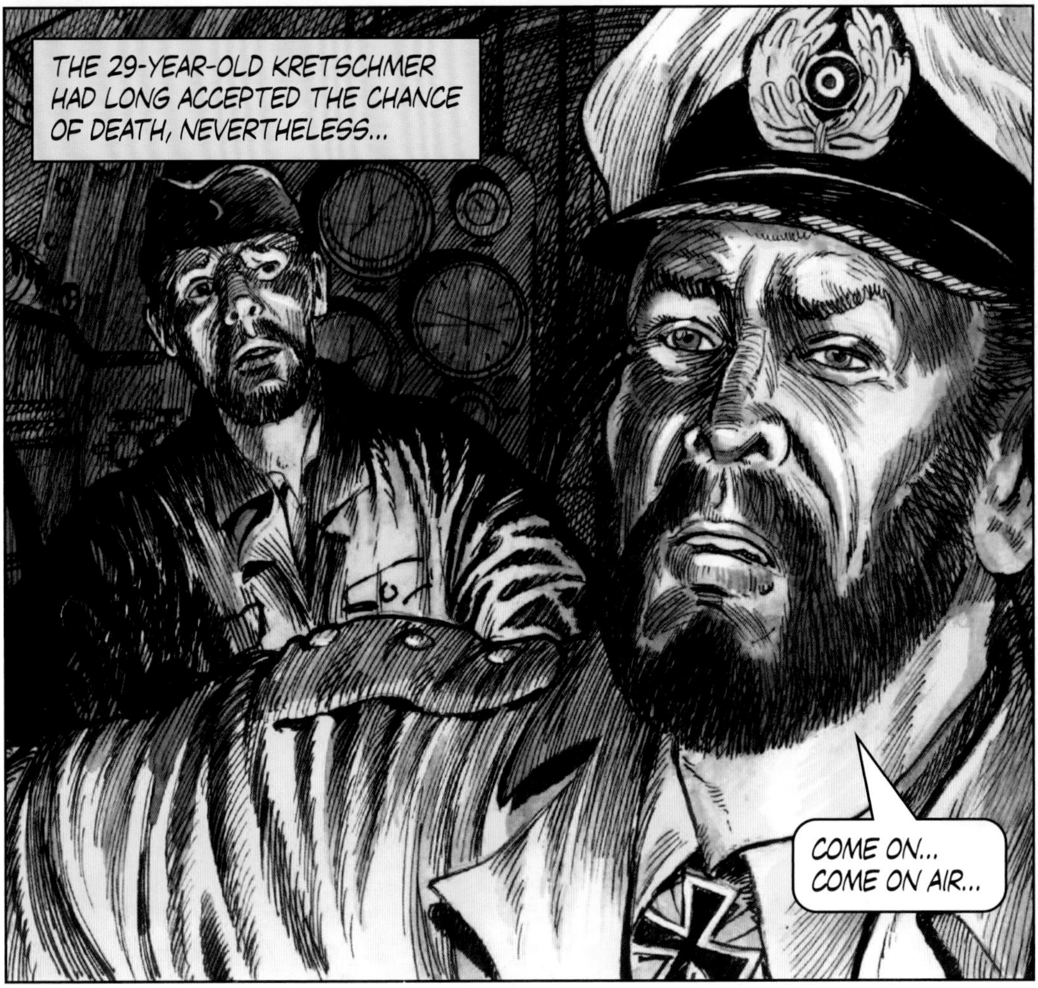
THE 29-YEAR-OLD KRETSCHMER HAD LONG ACCEPTED THE CHANCE OF DEATH, NEVERTHELESS...
COME ON... COME ON AIR...

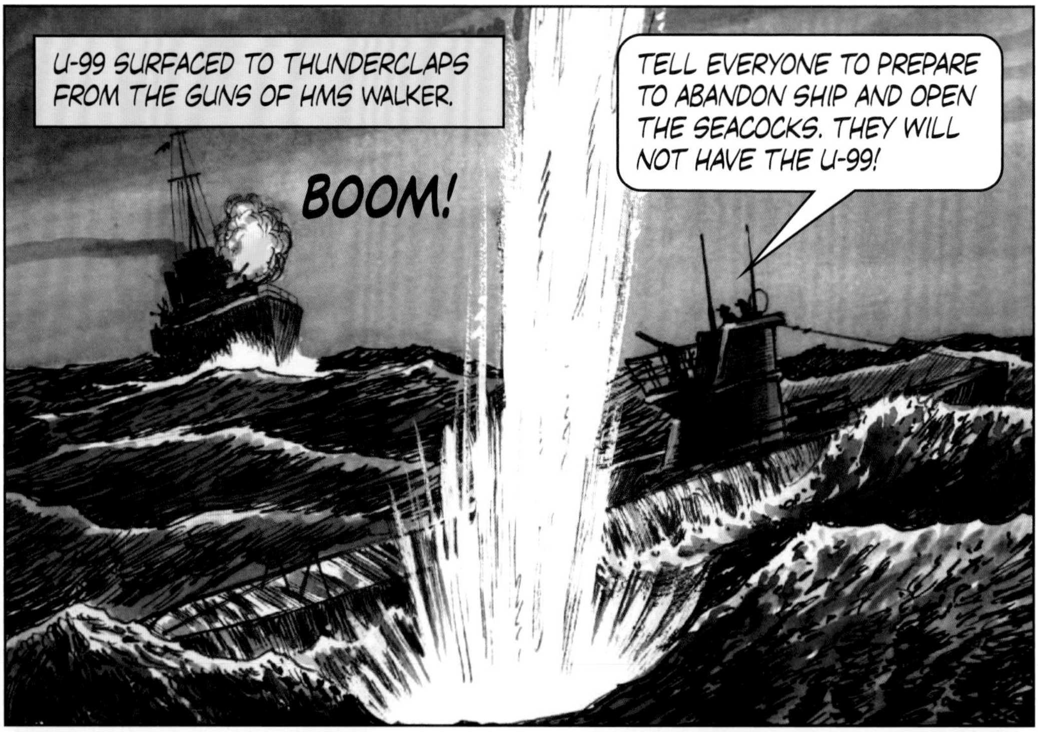
U-99 SURFACED TO THUNDERCLAPS FROM THE GUNS OF HMS WALKER.
BOOM!
TELL EVERYONE TO PREPARE TO ABANDON SHIP AND OPEN THE SEACOCKS. THEY WILL NOT HAVE THE U-99!

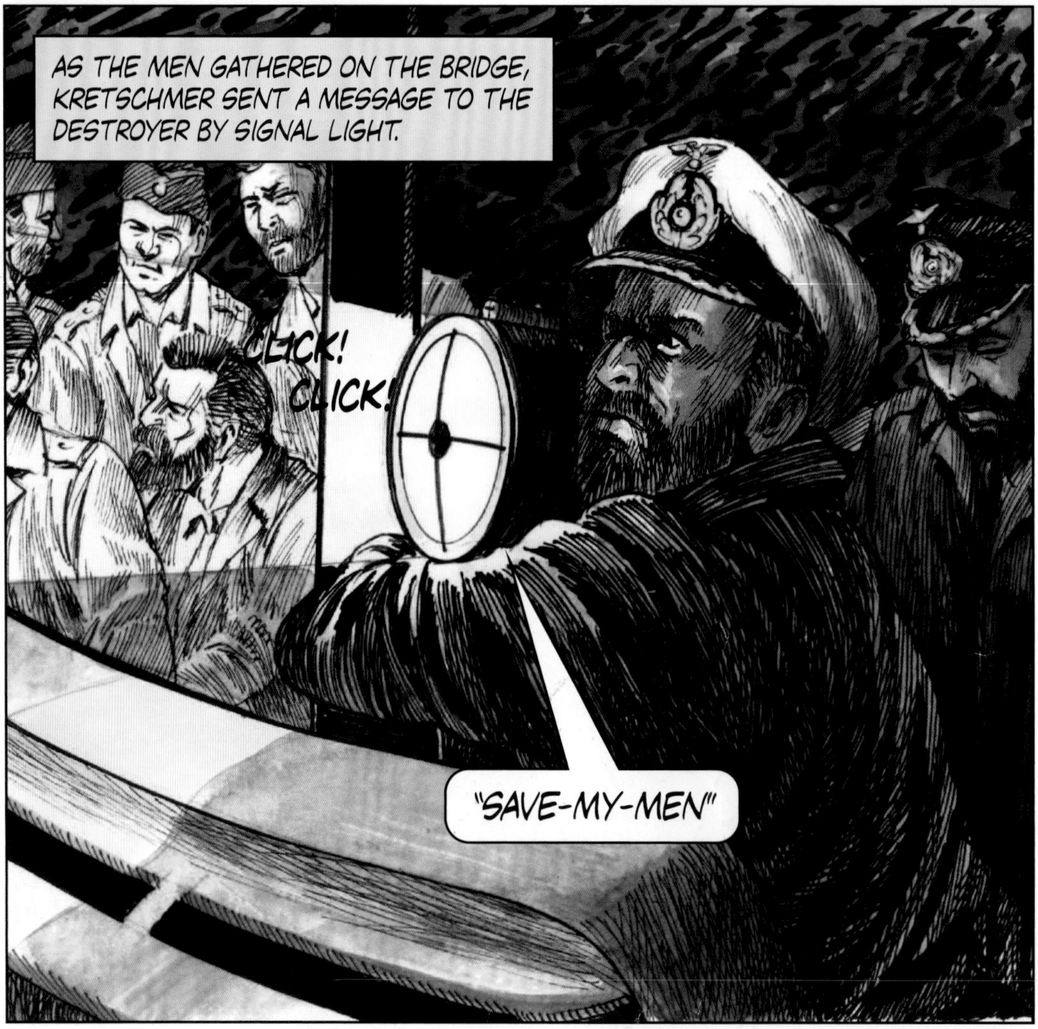
AS THE MEN GATHERED ON THE BRIDGE, KRETSCHMER SENT A MESSAGE TO THE DESTROYER BY SIGNAL LIGHT.
CLICK!
CLICK!
"SAVE-MY-MEN"

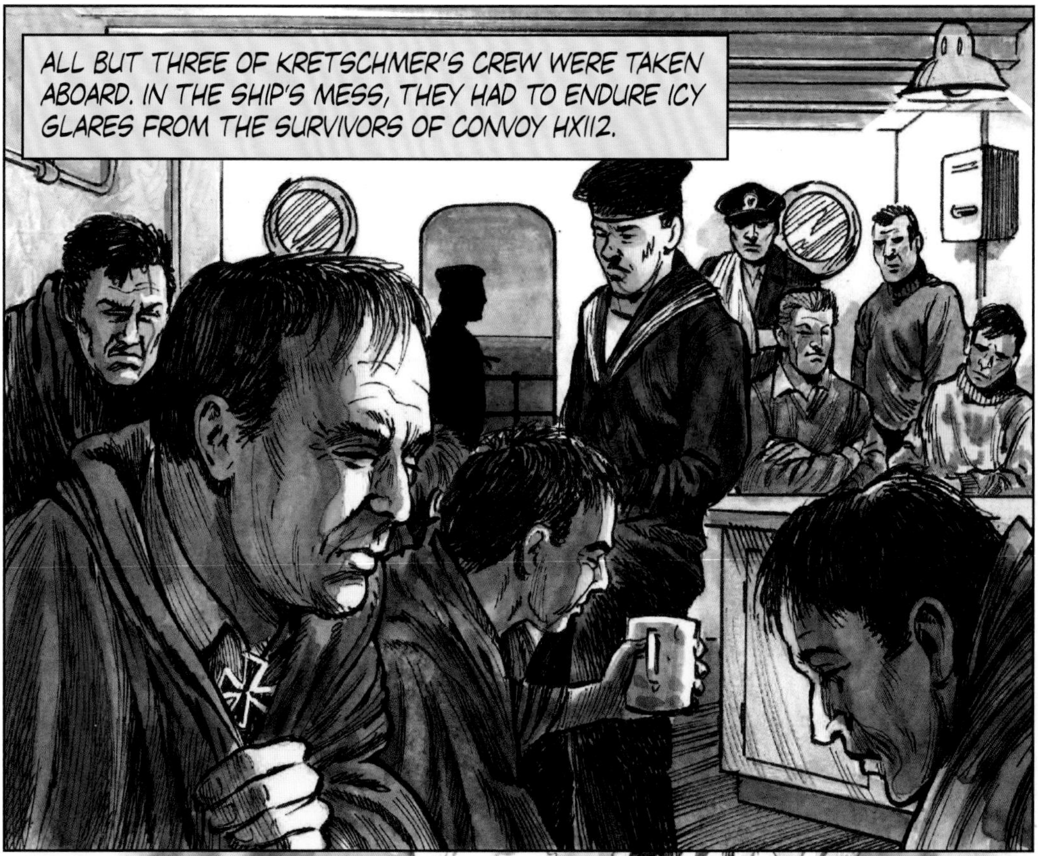
ALL BUT THREE OF KRETSCHMER'S CREW WERE TAKEN ABOARD. IN THE SHIP'S MESS, THEY HAD TO ENDURE ICY GLARES FROM THE SURVIVORS OF CONVOY HX112.

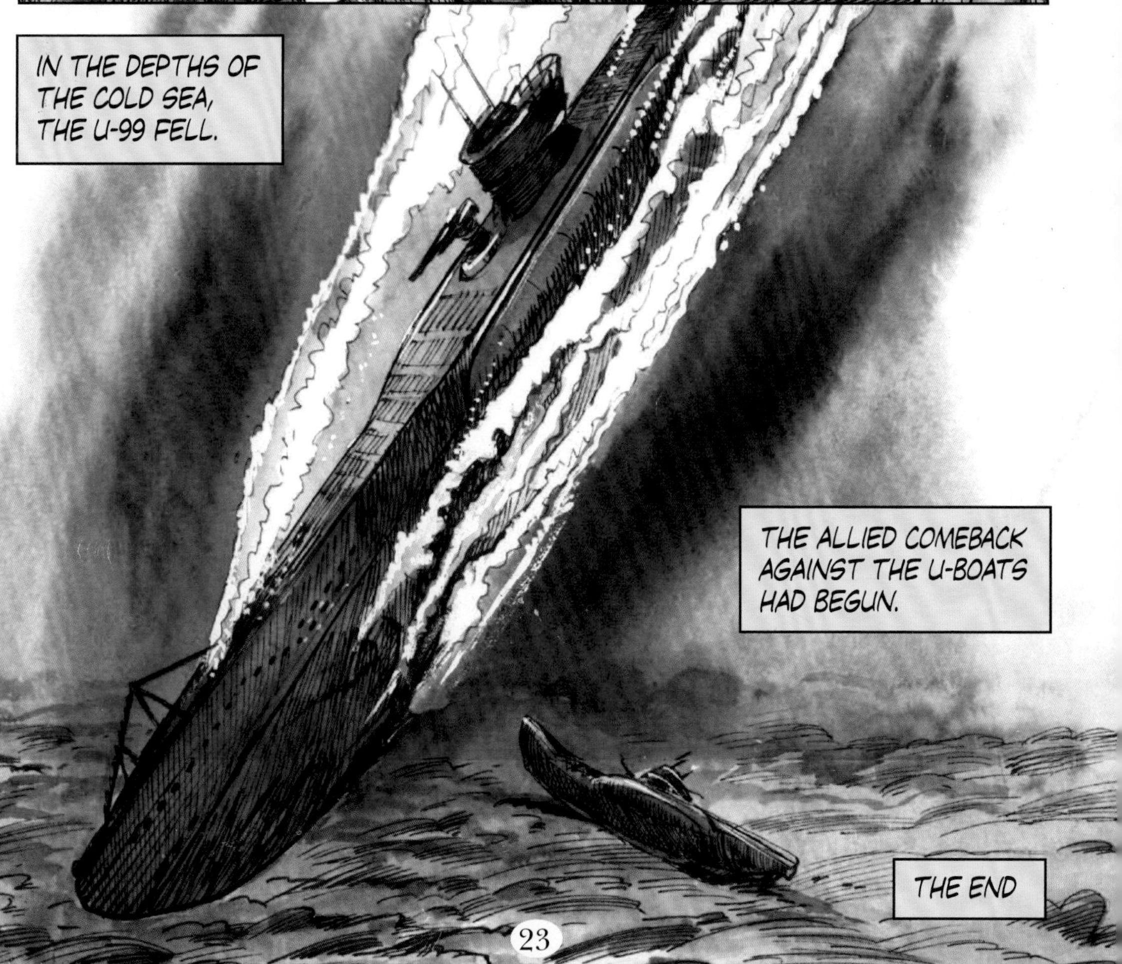
IN THE DEPTHS OF THE COLD SEA, THE U-99 FELL.
THE ALLIED COMEBACK AGAINST THE U-BOATS HAD BEGUN.
THE END

John Moffat

AIR ATTACK!—THE HUNT FOR THE *BISMARCK*

MAY 26, 1941

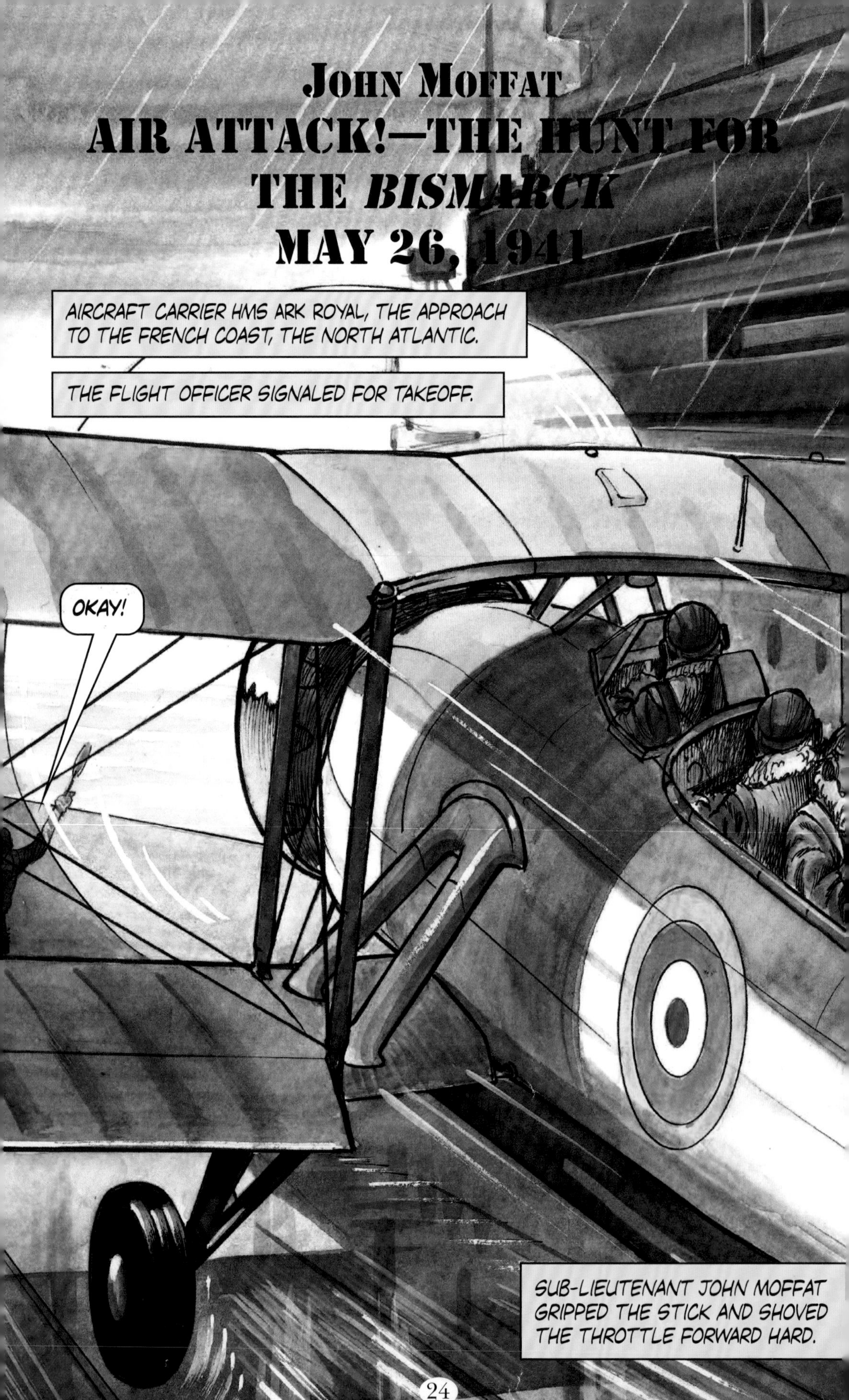
AIRCRAFT CARRIER HMS ARK ROYAL, THE APPROACH TO THE FRENCH COAST, THE NORTH ATLANTIC.
THE FLIGHT OFFICER SIGNALED FOR TAKEOFF.
OKAY!
SUB-LIEUTENANT JOHN MOFFAT GRIPPED THE STICK AND SHOVED THE THROTTLE FORWARD HARD.

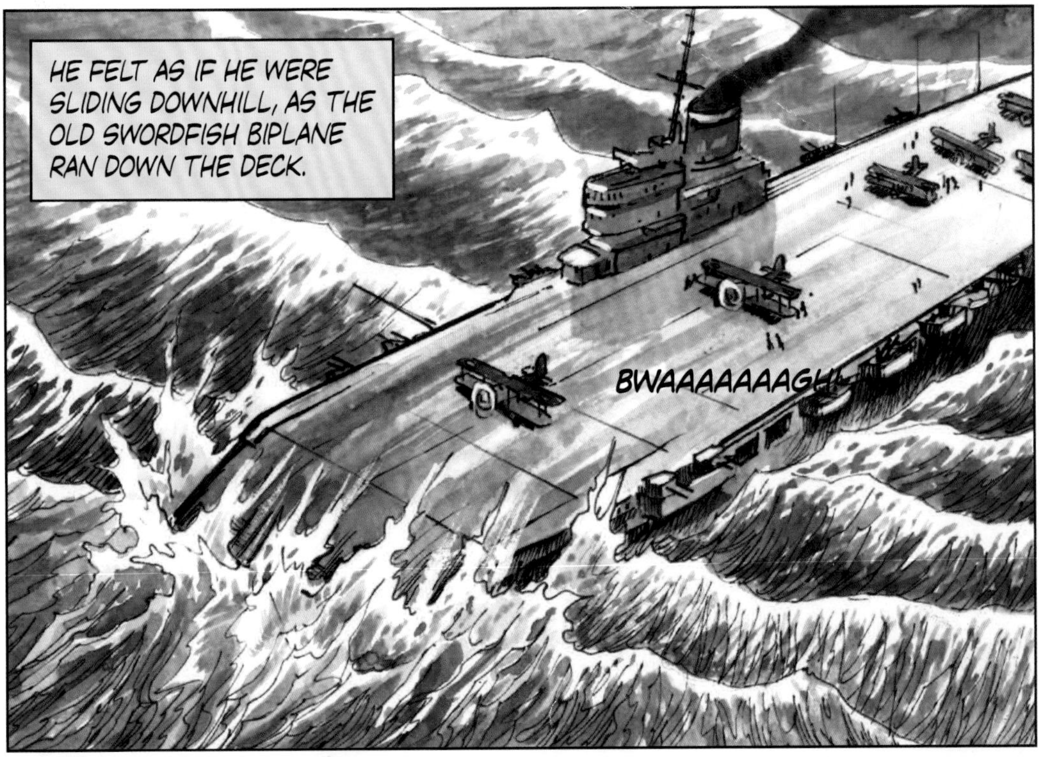
HE FELT AS IF HE WERE SLIDING DOWNHILL, AS THE OLD SWORDFISH BIPLANE RAN DOWN THE DECK.
BWAAAAAAAGH!

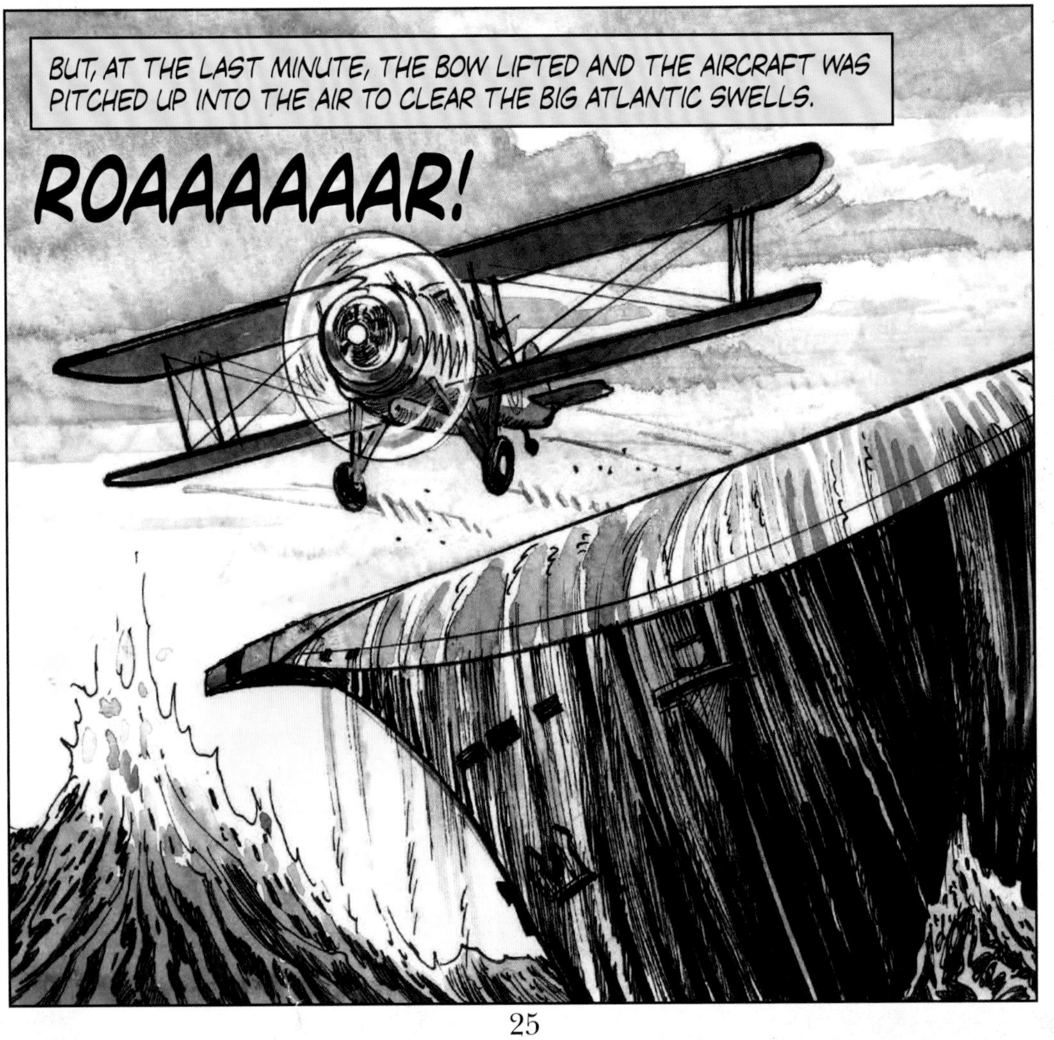
BUT, AT THE LAST MINUTE, THE BOW LIFTED AND THE AIRCRAFT WAS PITCHED UP INTO THE AIR TO CLEAR THE BIG ATLANTIC SWELLS.
ROAAAAAAR!

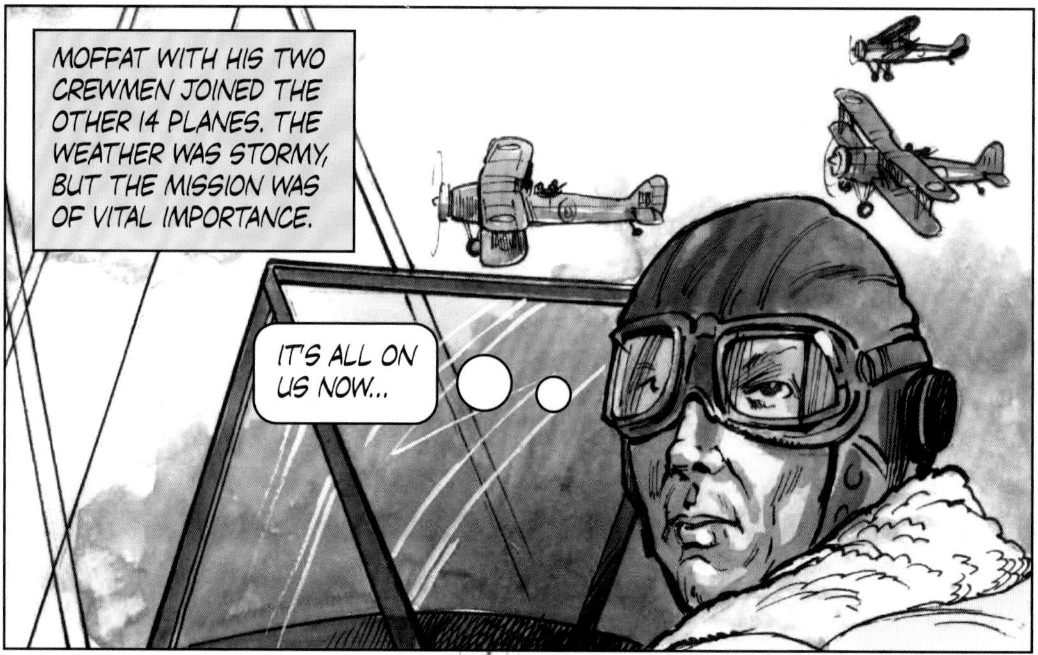
MOFFAT WITH HIS TWO CREWMEN JOINED THE OTHER 14 PLANES. THE WEATHER WAS STORMY, BUT THE MISSION WAS OF VITAL IMPORTANCE.
IT'S ALL ON US NOW...

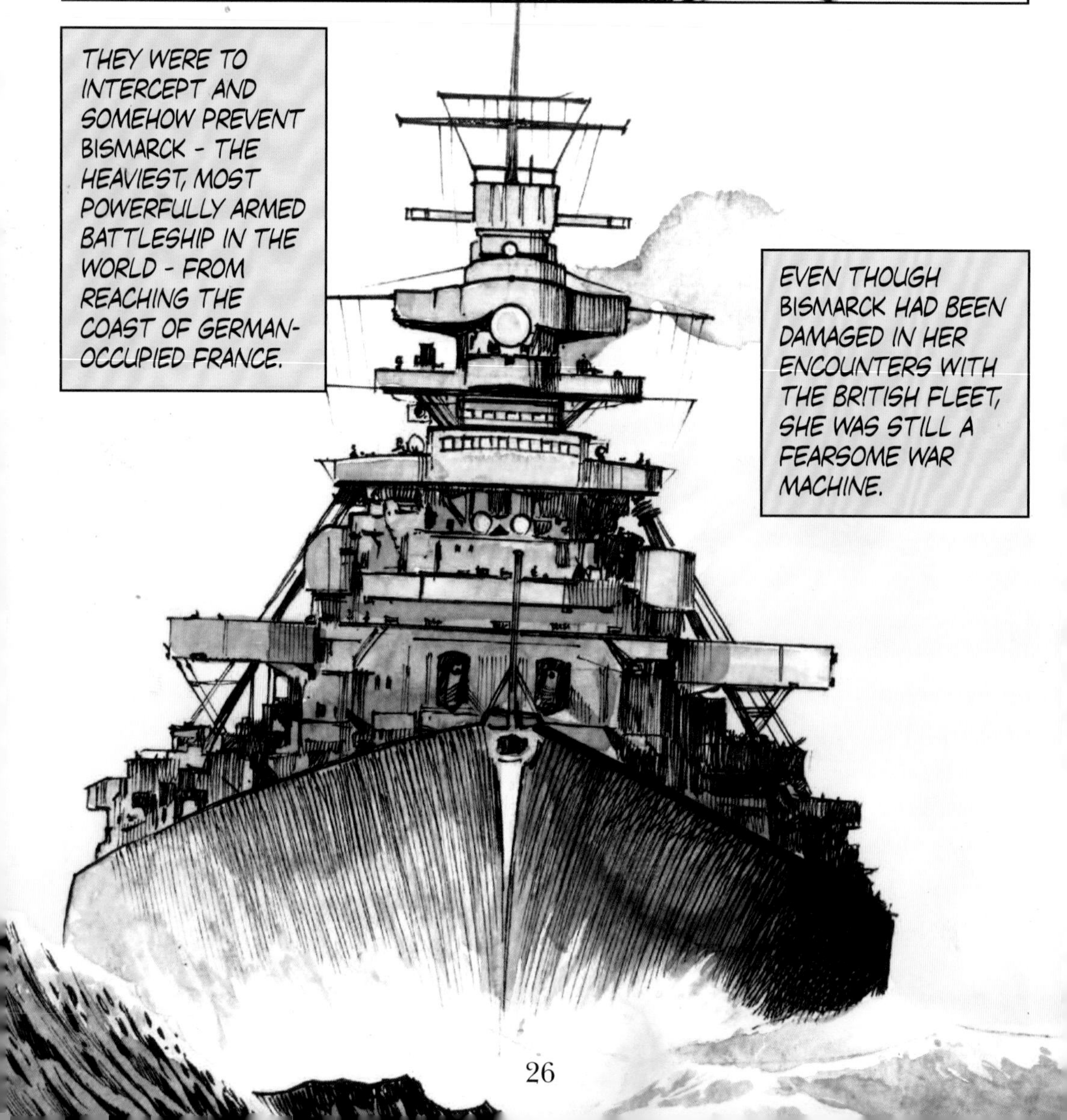
THEY WERE TO INTERCEPT AND SOMEHOW PREVENT BISMARCK - THE HEAVIEST, MOST POWERFULLY ARMED BATTLESHIP IN THE WORLD - FROM REACHING THE COAST OF GERMAN-OCCUPIED FRANCE.
EVEN THOUGH BISMARCK HAD BEEN DAMAGED IN HER ENCOUNTERS WITH THE BRITISH FLEET, SHE WAS STILL A FEARSOME WAR MACHINE.

JUST TWO DAYS EARLIER, DURING THE BATTLE OF THE DENMARK STRAIT, HER GUNS HAD SPOKEN.

KROOM!

HMS HOOD, PRIDE OF THE BRITISH FLEET, HAD BEEN BLOWN TO PIECES LEAVING JUST THREE SURVIVORS FROM A CREW OF 1400.

KABOOM!

THE DISASTER HAD ROCKED THE BRITISH PUBLIC. WINSTON CHURCHILL HAD DEMANDED THAT THE HOOD BE AVENGED. THE BISMARCK MUST BE SUNK!

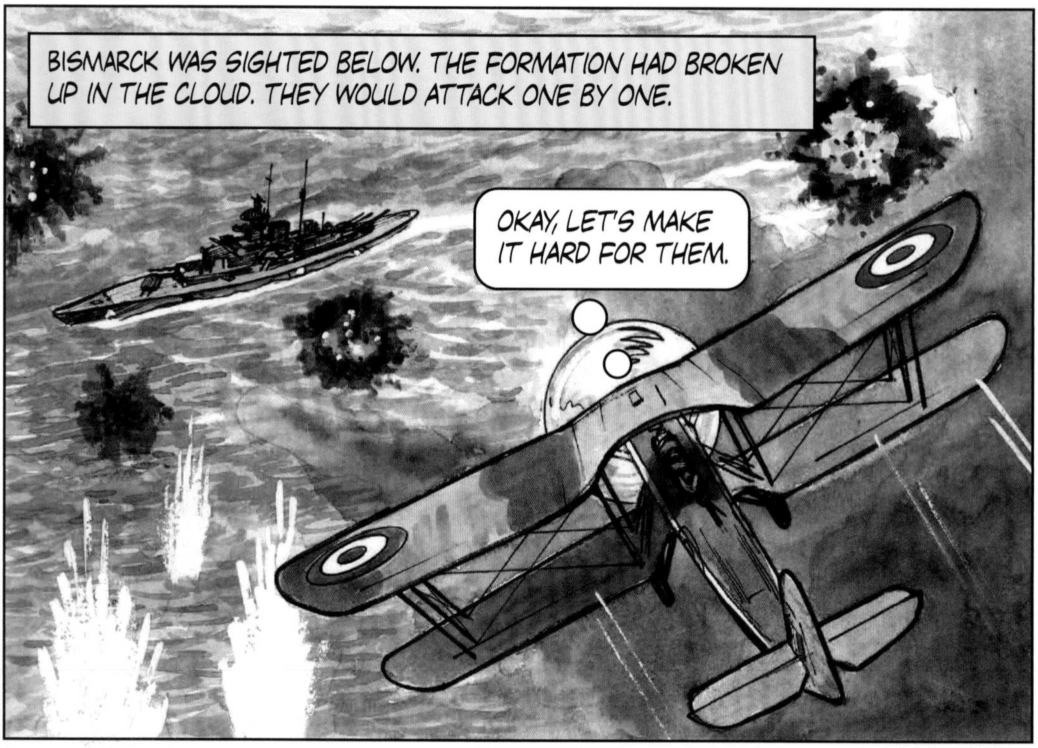
BISMARCK WAS SIGHTED BELOW. THE FORMATION HAD BROKEN UP IN THE CLOUD. THEY WOULD ATTACK ONE BY ONE.
OKAY, LET'S MAKE IT HARD FOR THEM.

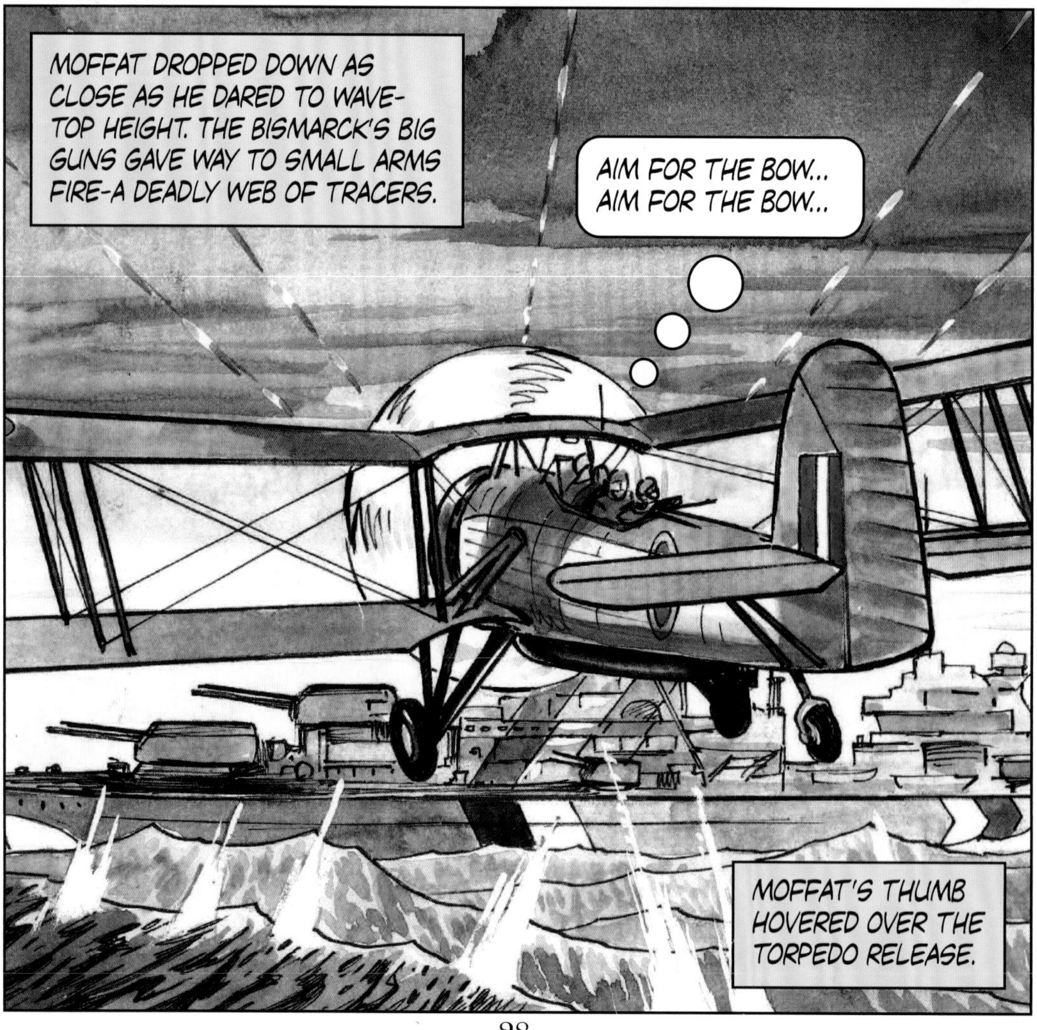
MOFFAT DROPPED DOWN AS CLOSE AS HE DARED TO WAVE-TOP HEIGHT. THE BISMARCK'S BIG GUNS GAVE WAY TO SMALL ARMS FIRE-A DEADLY WEB OF TRACERS.
AIM FOR THE BOW... AIM FOR THE BOW...
MOFFAT'S THUMB HOVERED OVER THE TORPEDO RELEASE.

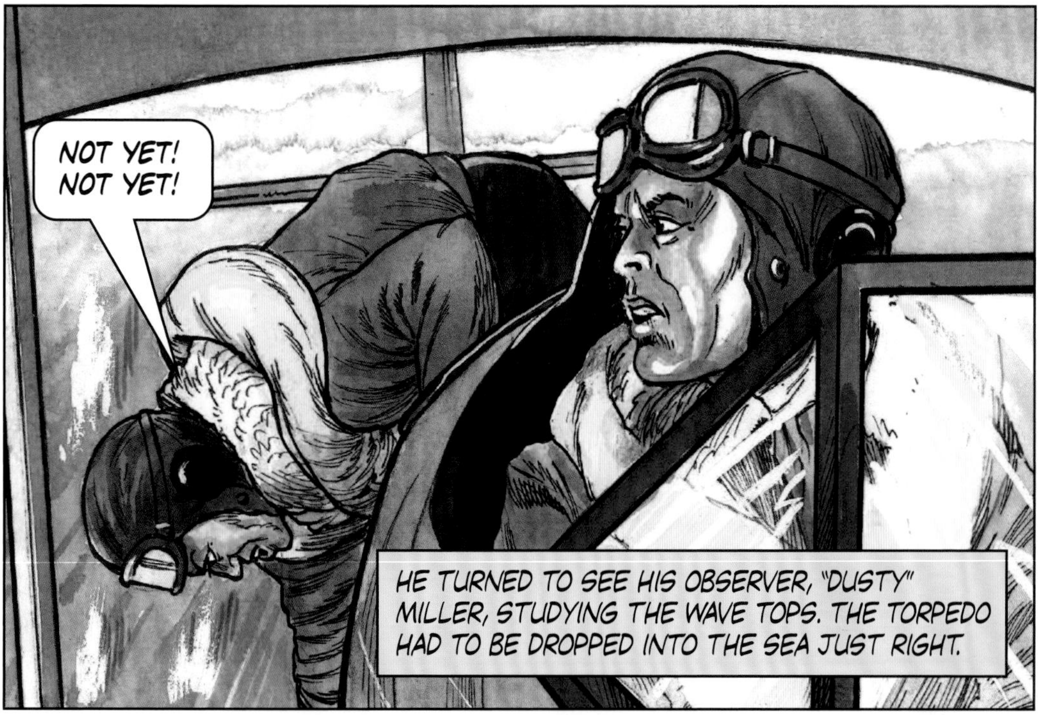
NOT YET! NOT YET!
HE TURNED TO SEE HIS OBSERVER, "DUSTY" MILLER, STUDYING THE WAVE TOPS. THE TORPEDO HAD TO BE DROPPED INTO THE SEA JUST RIGHT.

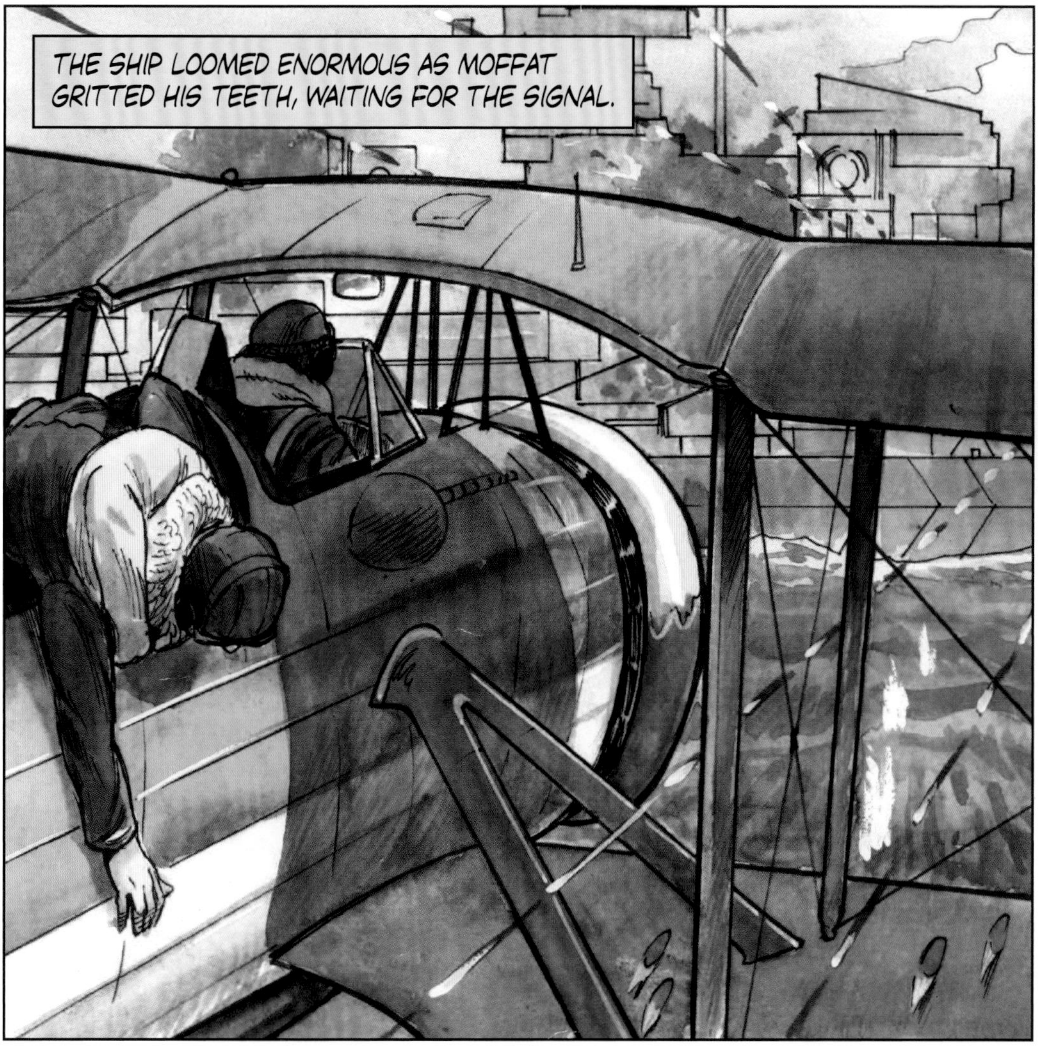
THE SHIP LOOMED ENORMOUS AS MOFFAT GRITTED HIS TEETH, WAITING FOR THE SIGNAL.

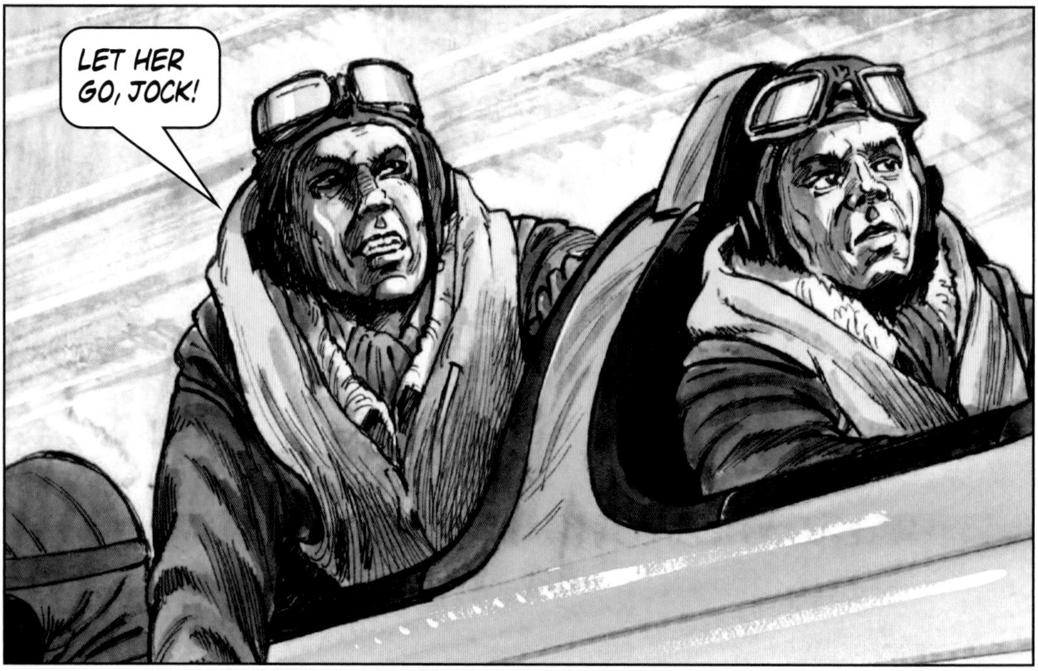
LET HER GO, JOCK!

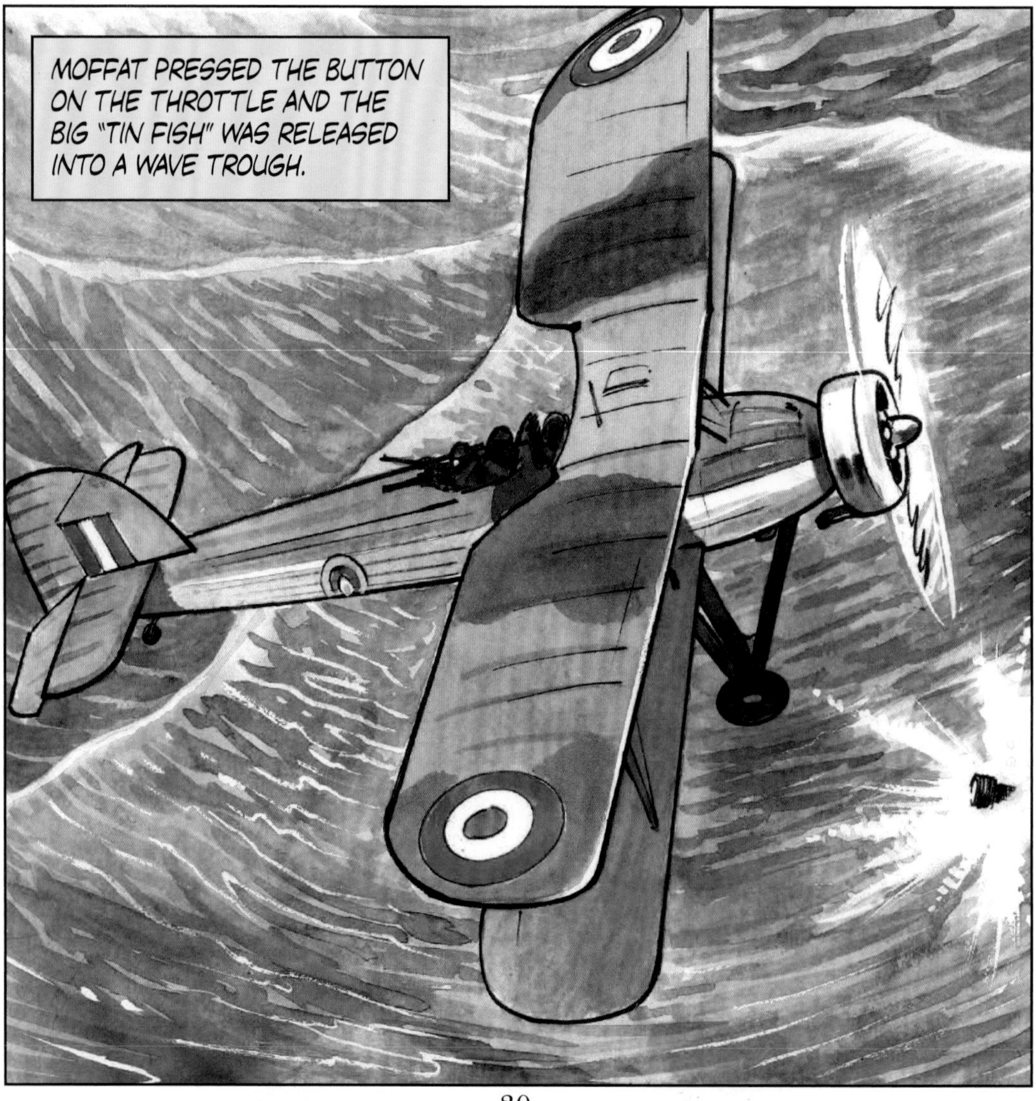
MOFFAT PRESSED THE BUTTON ON THE THROTTLE AND THE BIG "TIN FISH" WAS RELEASED INTO A WAVE TROUGH.

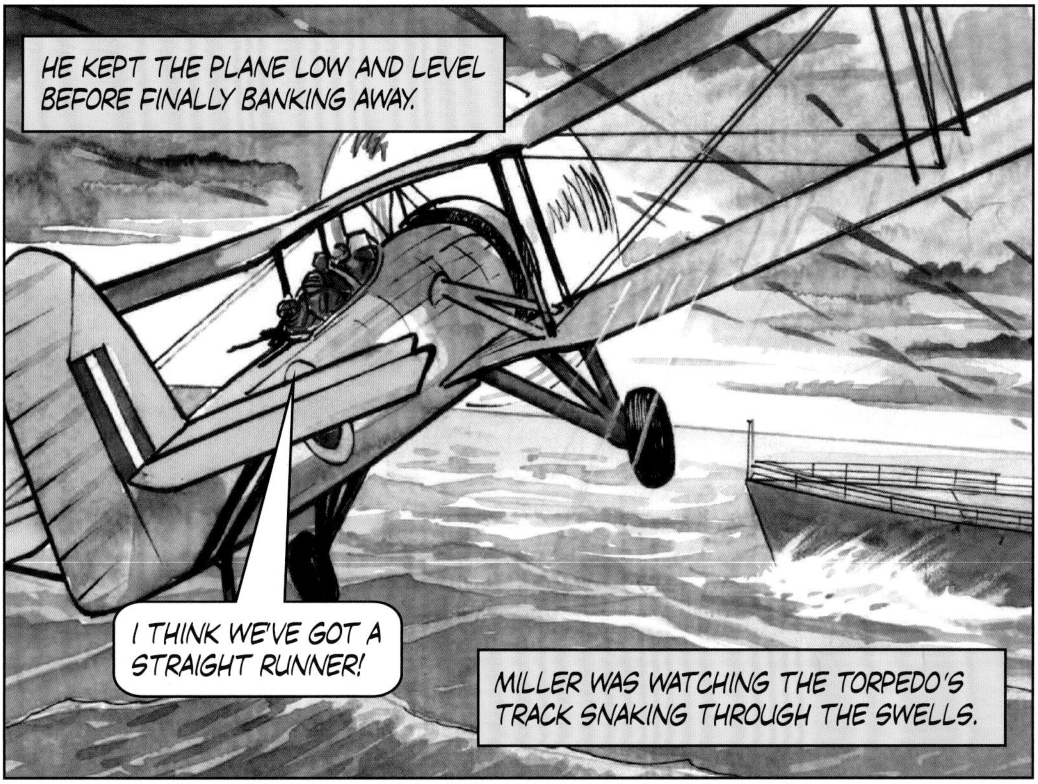
HE KEPT THE PLANE LOW AND LEVEL BEFORE FINALLY BANKING AWAY.
I THINK WE'VE GOT A STRAIGHT RUNNER!
MILLER WAS WATCHING THE TORPEDO'S TRACK SNAKING THROUGH THE SWELLS.

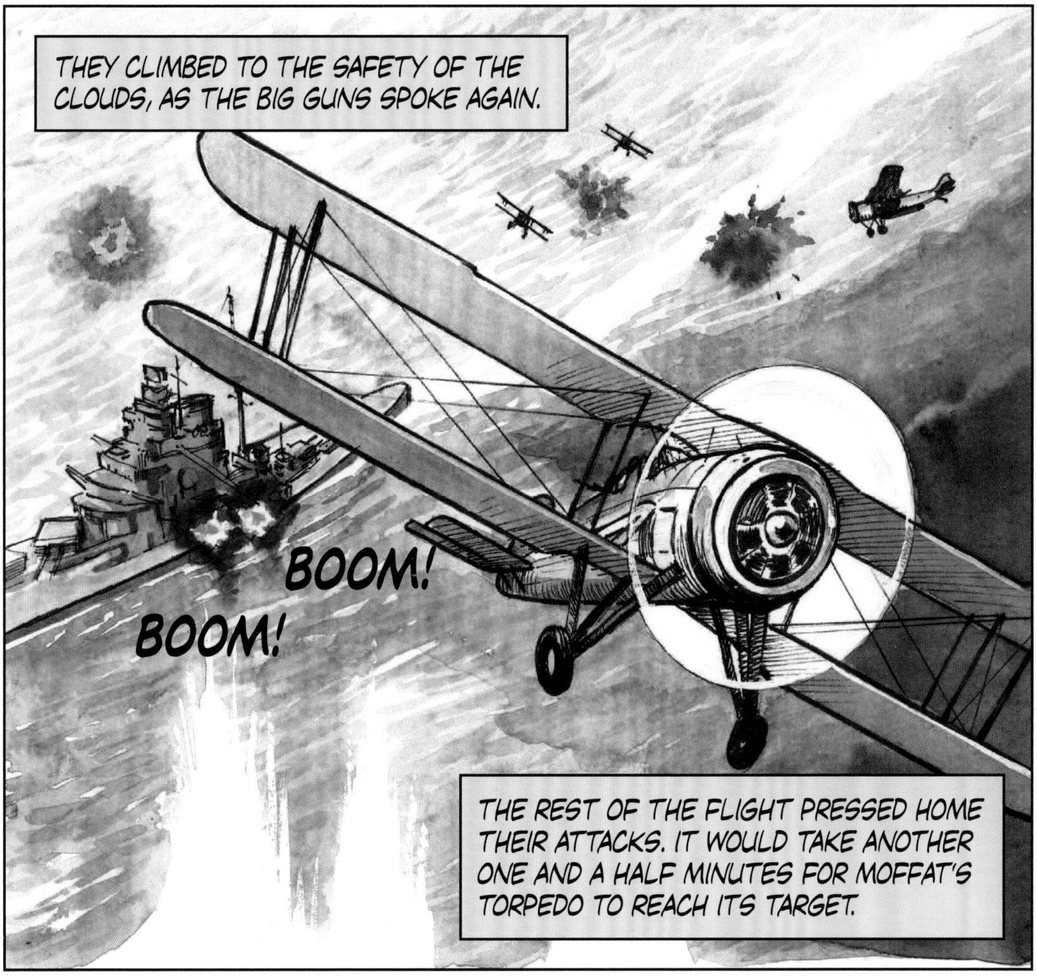
THEY CLIMBED TO THE SAFETY OF THE CLOUDS, AS THE BIG GUNS SPOKE AGAIN.
BOOM!
BOOM!
THE REST OF THE FLIGHT PRESSED HOME THEIR ATTACKS. IT WOULD TAKE ANOTHER ONE AND A HALF MINUTES FOR MOFFAT'S TORPEDO TO REACH ITS TARGET.

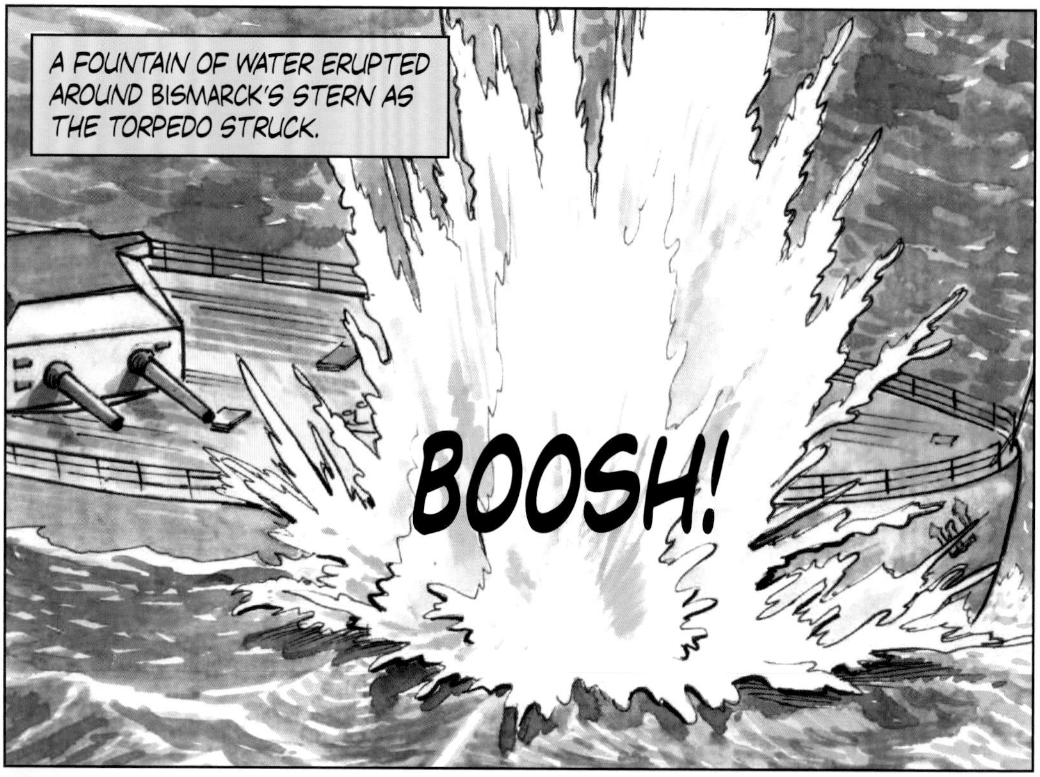
A FOUNTAIN OF WATER ERUPTED AROUND BISMARCK'S STERN AS THE TORPEDO STRUCK.
BOOSH!

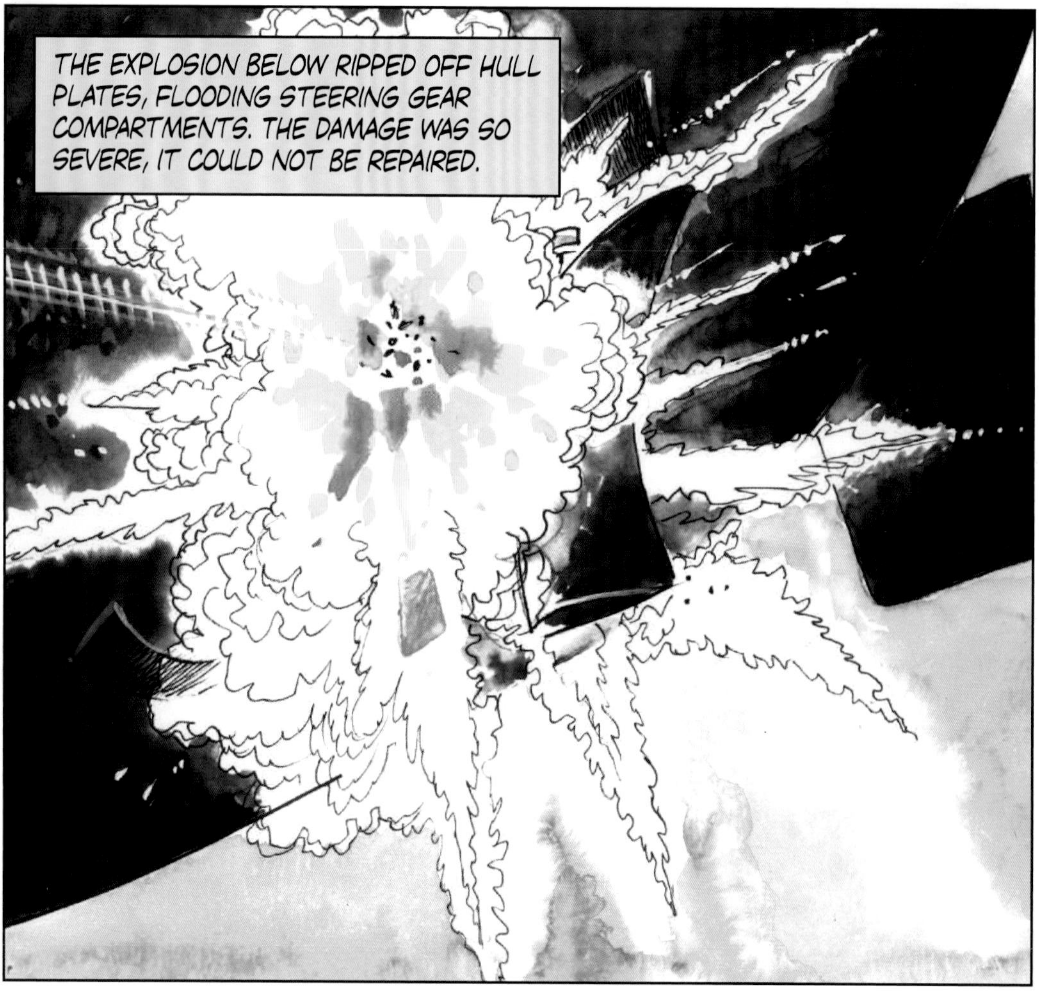
THE EXPLOSION BELOW RIPPED OFF HULL PLATES, FLOODING STEERING GEAR COMPARTMENTS. THE DAMAGE WAS SO SEVERE, IT COULD NOT BE REPAIRED.

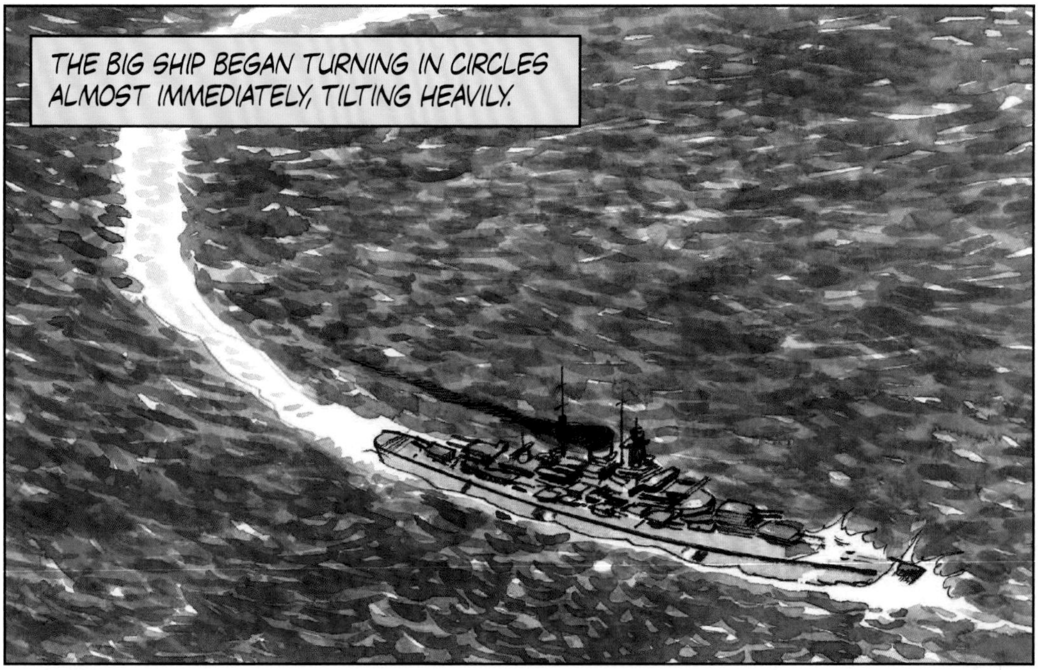
THE BIG SHIP BEGAN TURNING IN CIRCLES ALMOST IMMEDIATELY, TILTING HEAVILY.

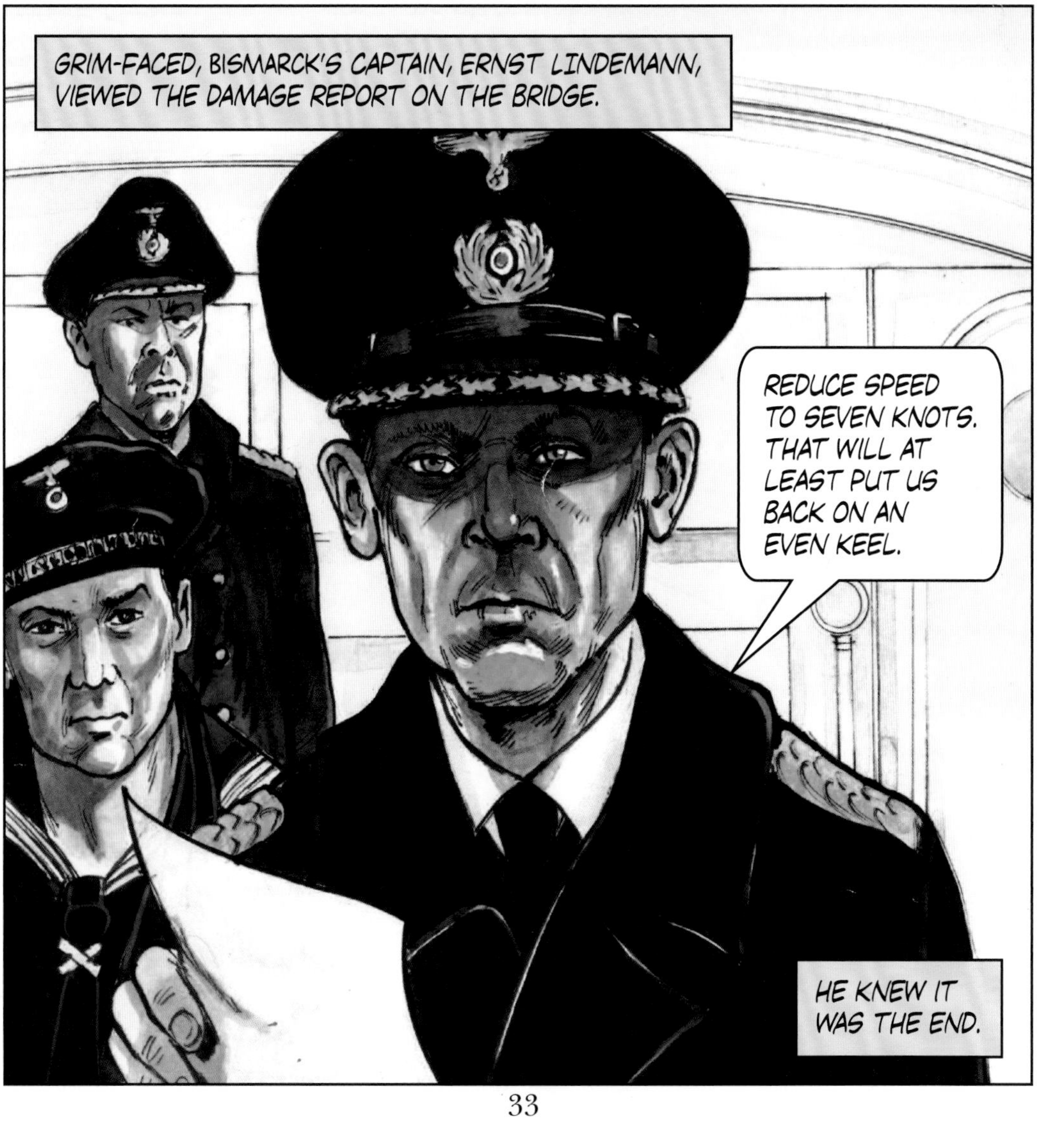
GRIM-FACED, BISMARCK'S CAPTAIN, ERNST LINDEMANN, VIEWED THE DAMAGE REPORT ON THE BRIDGE.
REDUCE SPEED TO SEVEN KNOTS. THAT WILL AT LEAST PUT US BACK ON AN EVEN KEEL.
HE KNEW IT WAS THE END.

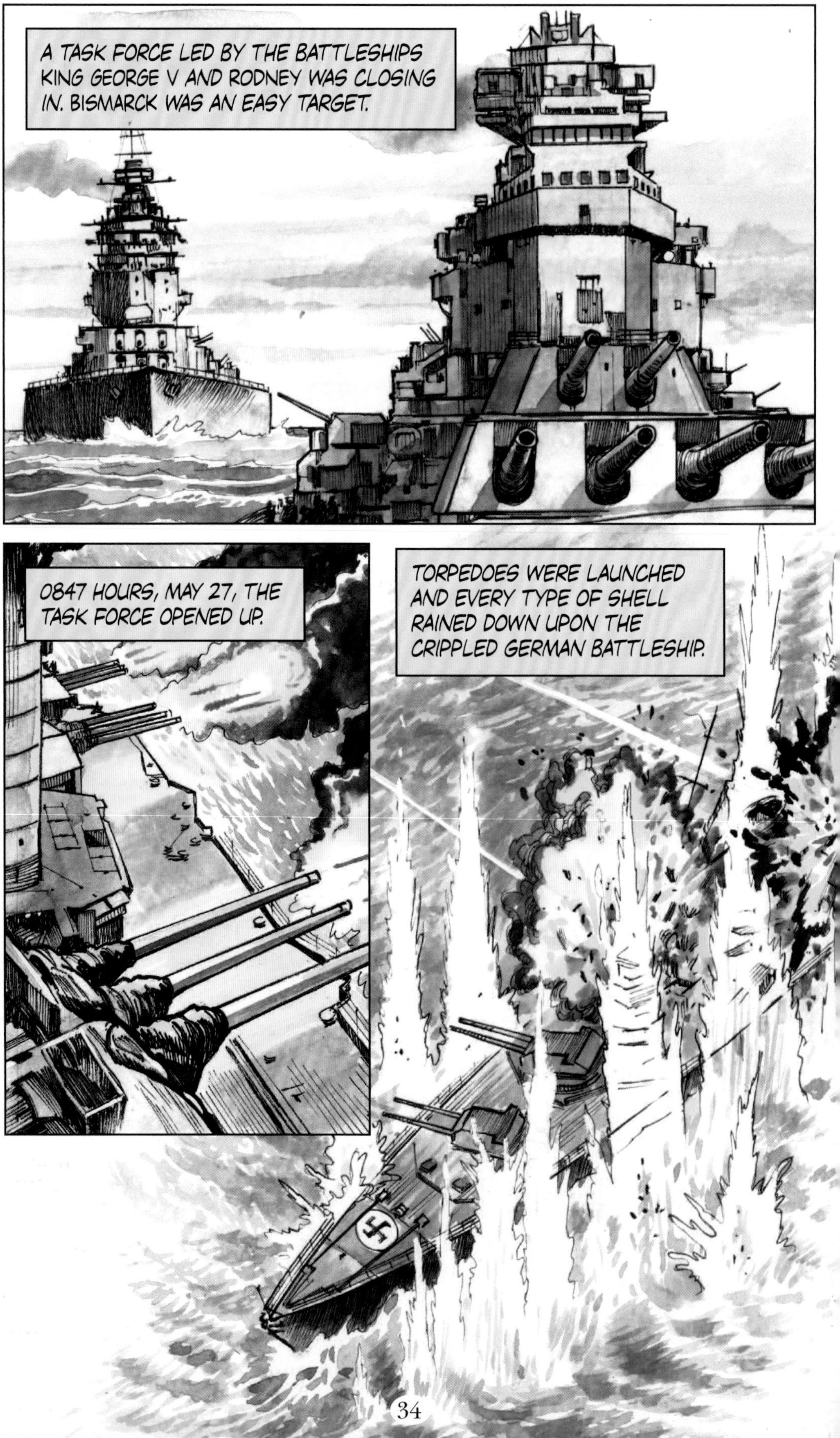
A TASK FORCE LED BY THE BATTLESHIPS KING GEORGE V AND RODNEY WAS CLOSING IN. BISMARCK WAS AN EASY TARGET.
0847 HOURS, MAY 27, THE TASK FORCE OPENED UP.
TORPEDOES WERE LAUNCHED AND EVERY TYPE OF SHELL RAINED DOWN UPON THE CRIPPLED GERMAN BATTLESHIP.

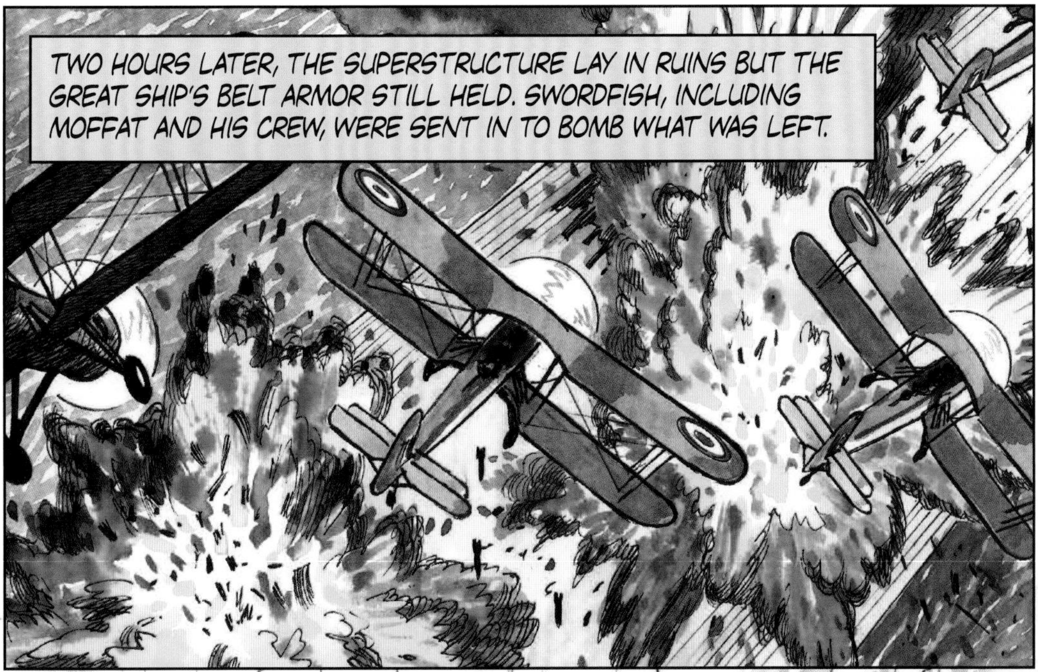
TWO HOURS LATER, THE SUPERSTRUCTURE LAY IN RUINS BUT THE GREAT SHIP'S BELT ARMOR STILL HELD. SWORDFISH, INCLUDING MOFFAT AND HIS CREW, WERE SENT IN TO BOMB WHAT WAS LEFT.

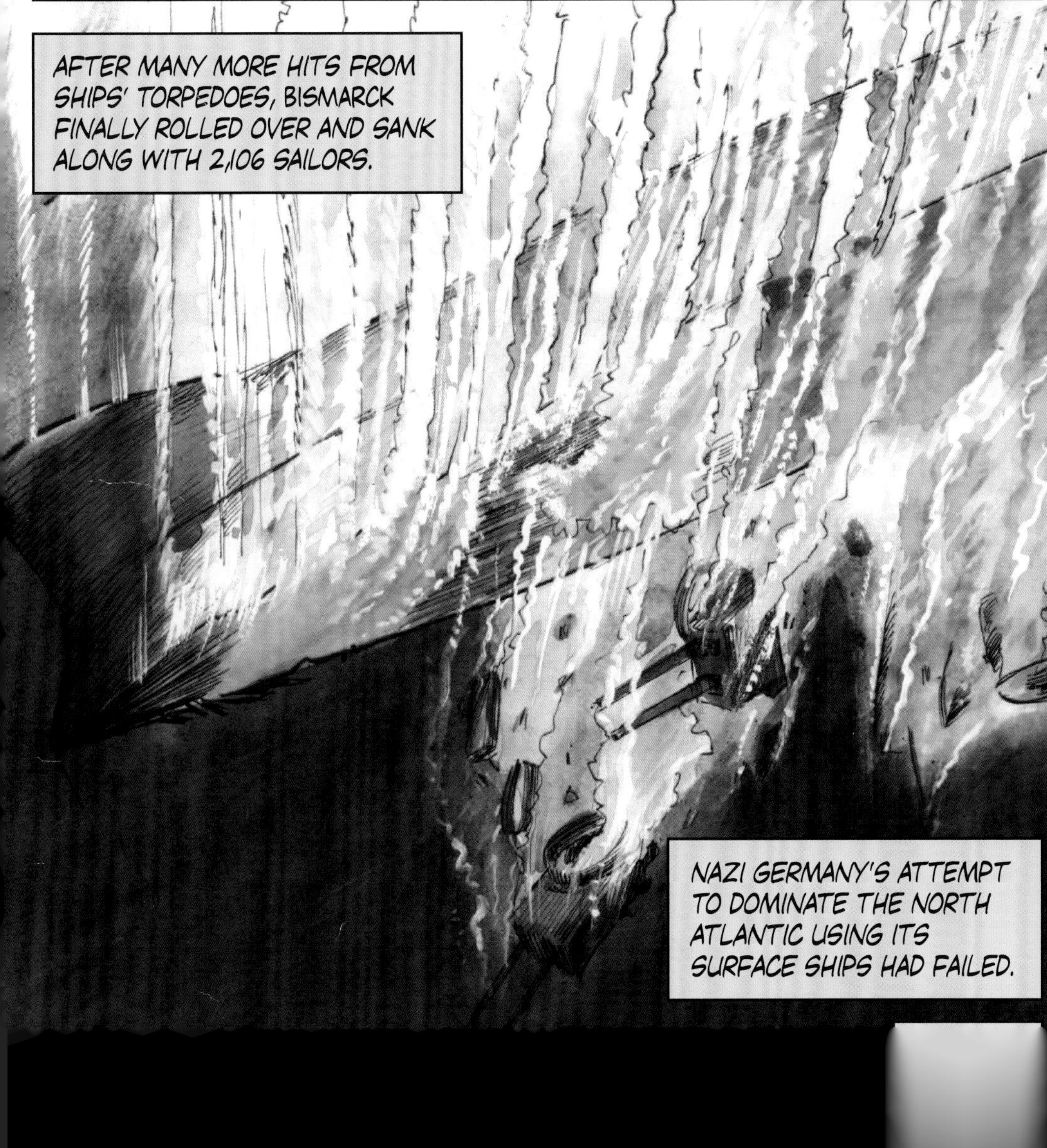
AFTER MANY MORE HITS FROM SHIPS' TORPEDOES, BISMARCK FINALLY ROLLED OVER AND SANK ALONG WITH 2,106 SAILORS.
NAZI GERMANY'S ATTEMPT TO DOMINATE THE NORTH ATLANTIC USING ITS SURFACE SHIPS HAD FAILED.

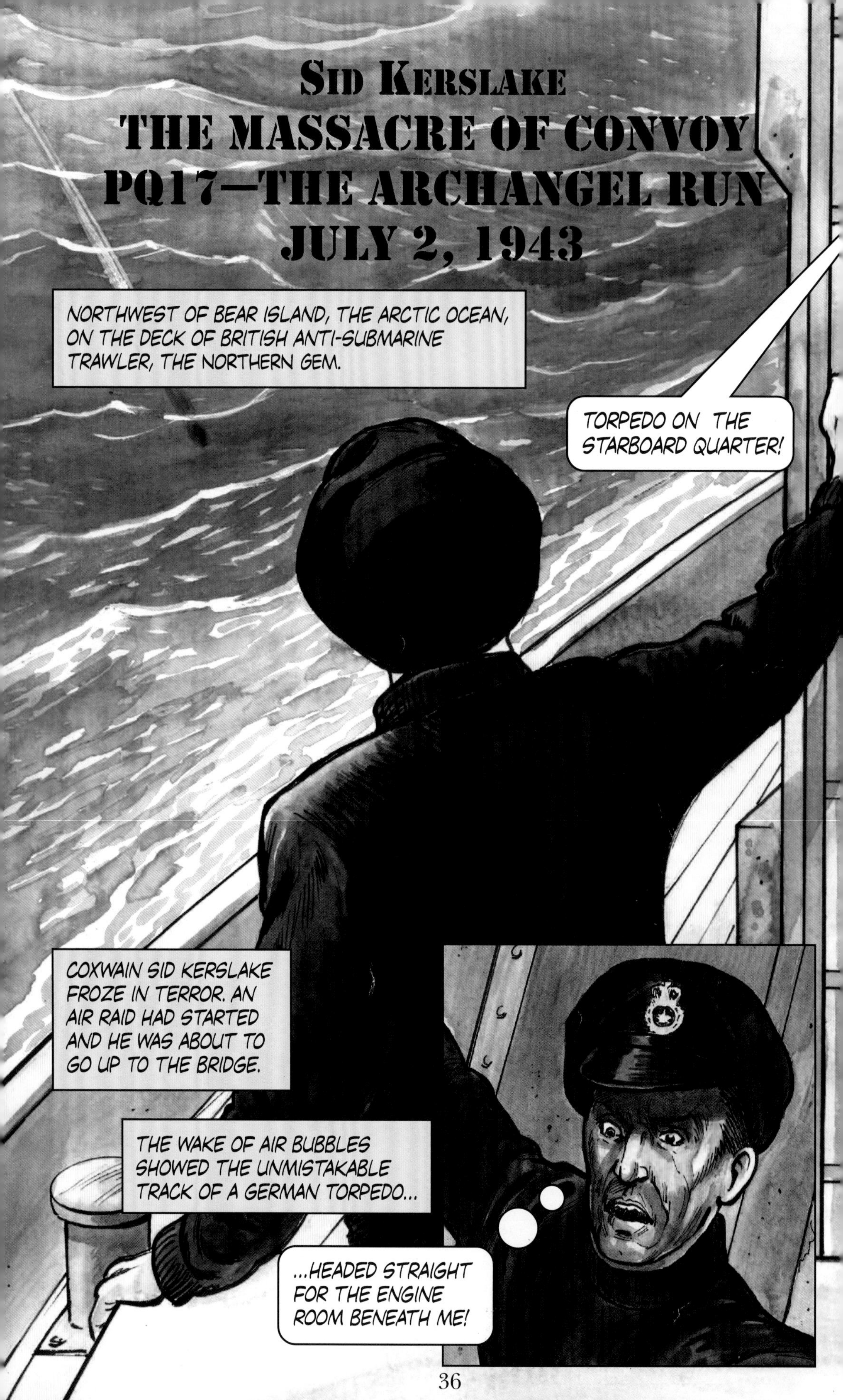
SID KERSLAKE
THE MASSACRE OF CONVOY PQ17—THE ARCHANGEL RUN
JULY 2, 1943
NORTHWEST OF BEAR ISLAND, THE ARCTIC OCEAN, ON THE DECK OF BRITISH ANTI-SUBMARINE TRAWLER, THE NORTHERN GEM.
TORPEDO ON THE STARBOARD QUARTER!
COXWAIN SID KERSLAKE FROZE IN TERROR. AN AIR RAID HAD STARTED AND HE WAS ABOUT TO GO UP TO THE BRIDGE.
THE WAKE OF AIR BUBBLES SHOWED THE UNMISTAKABLE TRACK OF A GERMAN TORPEDO...
...HEADED STRAIGHT FOR THE ENGINE ROOM BENEATH ME!

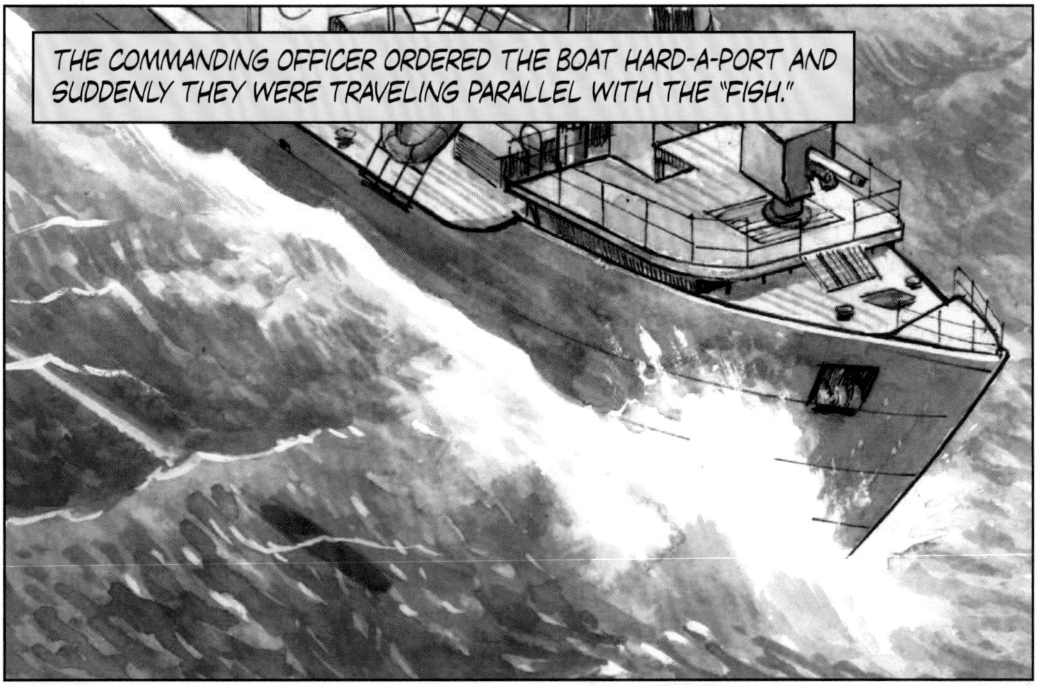
THE COMMANDING OFFICER ORDERED THE BOAT HARD-A-PORT AND SUDDENLY THEY WERE TRAVELING PARALLEL WITH THE "FISH."

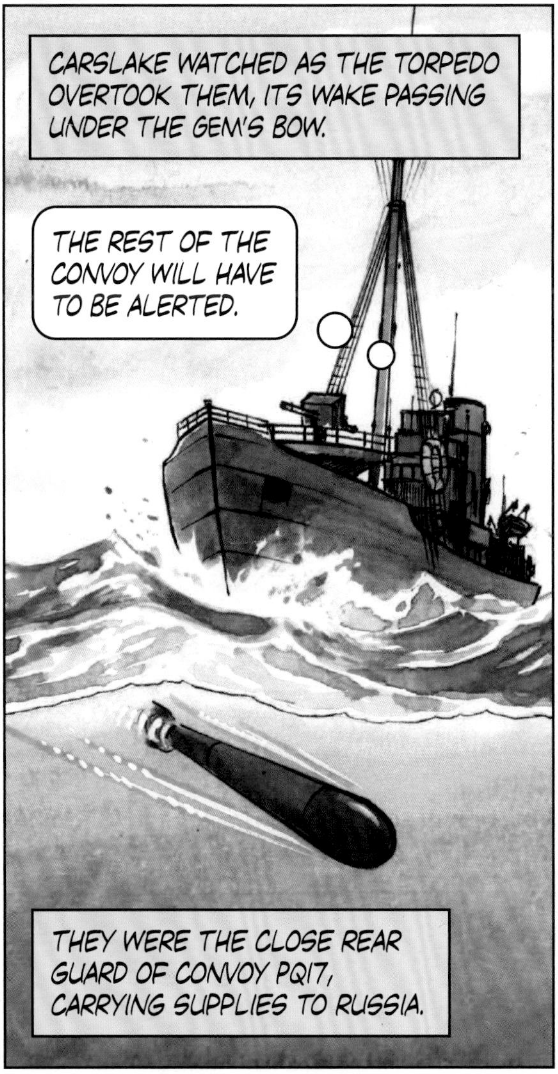
CARSLAKE WATCHED AS THE TORPEDO OVERTOOK THEM, ITS WAKE PASSING UNDER THE GEM'S BOW.
THE REST OF THE CONVOY WILL HAVE TO BE ALERTED.
THEY WERE THE CLOSE REAR GUARD OF CONVOY PQ17, CARRYING SUPPLIES TO RUSSIA.

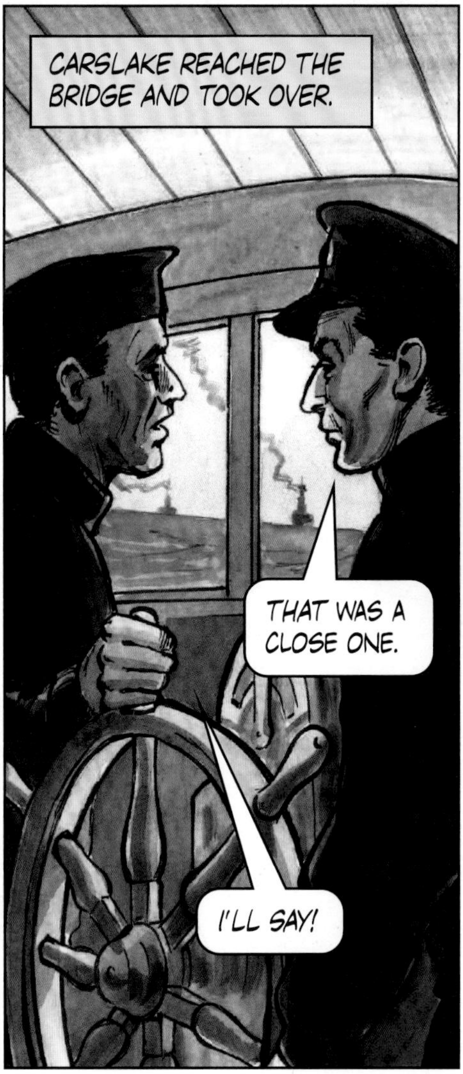
CARSLAKE REACHED THE BRIDGE AND TOOK OVER.
THAT WAS A CLOSE ONE.
I'LL SAY!

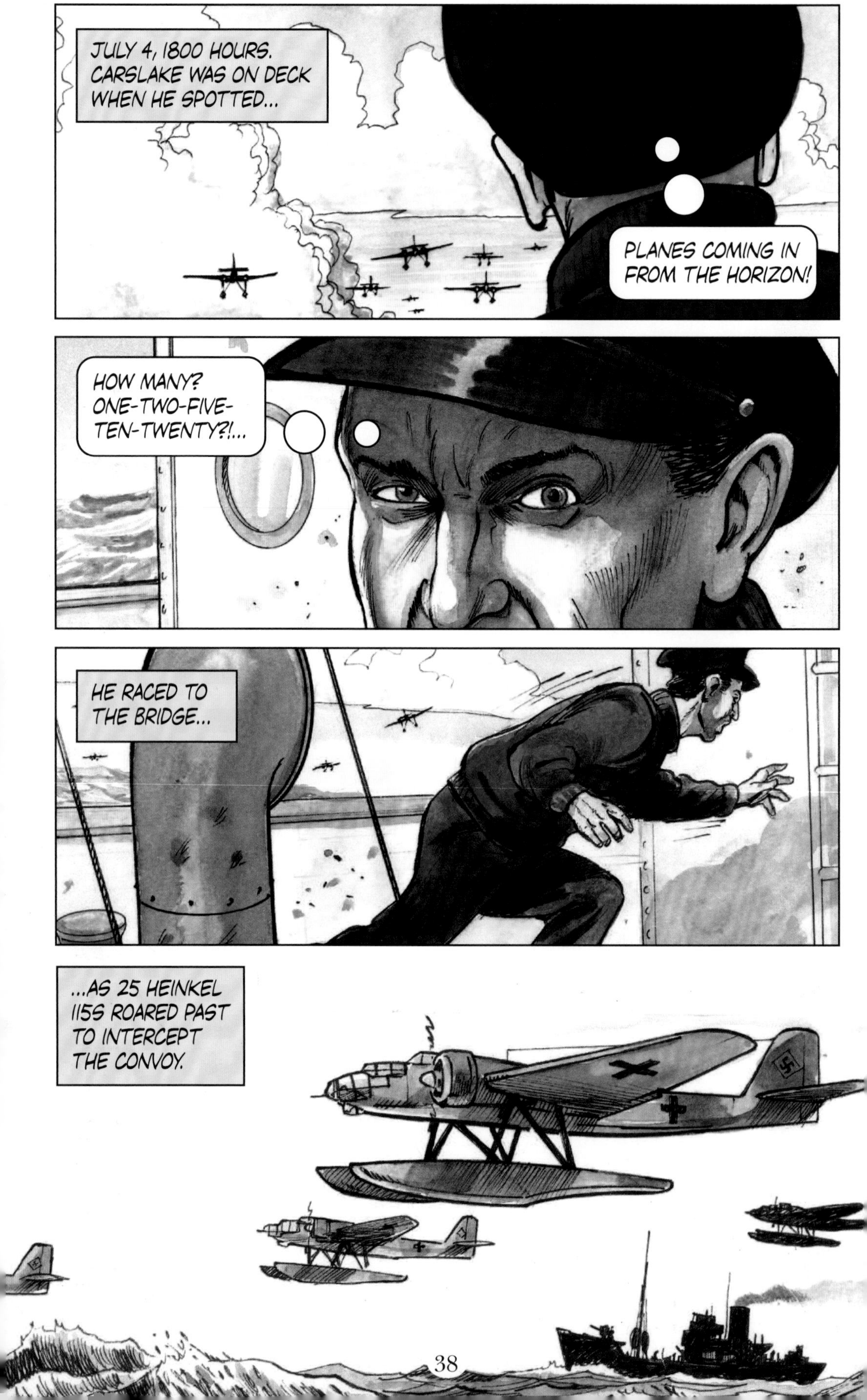
JULY 4, 1800 HOURS. CARSLAKE WAS ON DECK WHEN HE SPOTTED...
PLANES COMING IN FROM THE HORIZON!
HOW MANY? ONE-TWO-FIVE-TEN-TWENTY?!...
HE RACED TO THE BRIDGE...
...AS 25 HEINKEL 115S ROARED PAST TO INTERCEPT THE CONVOY.

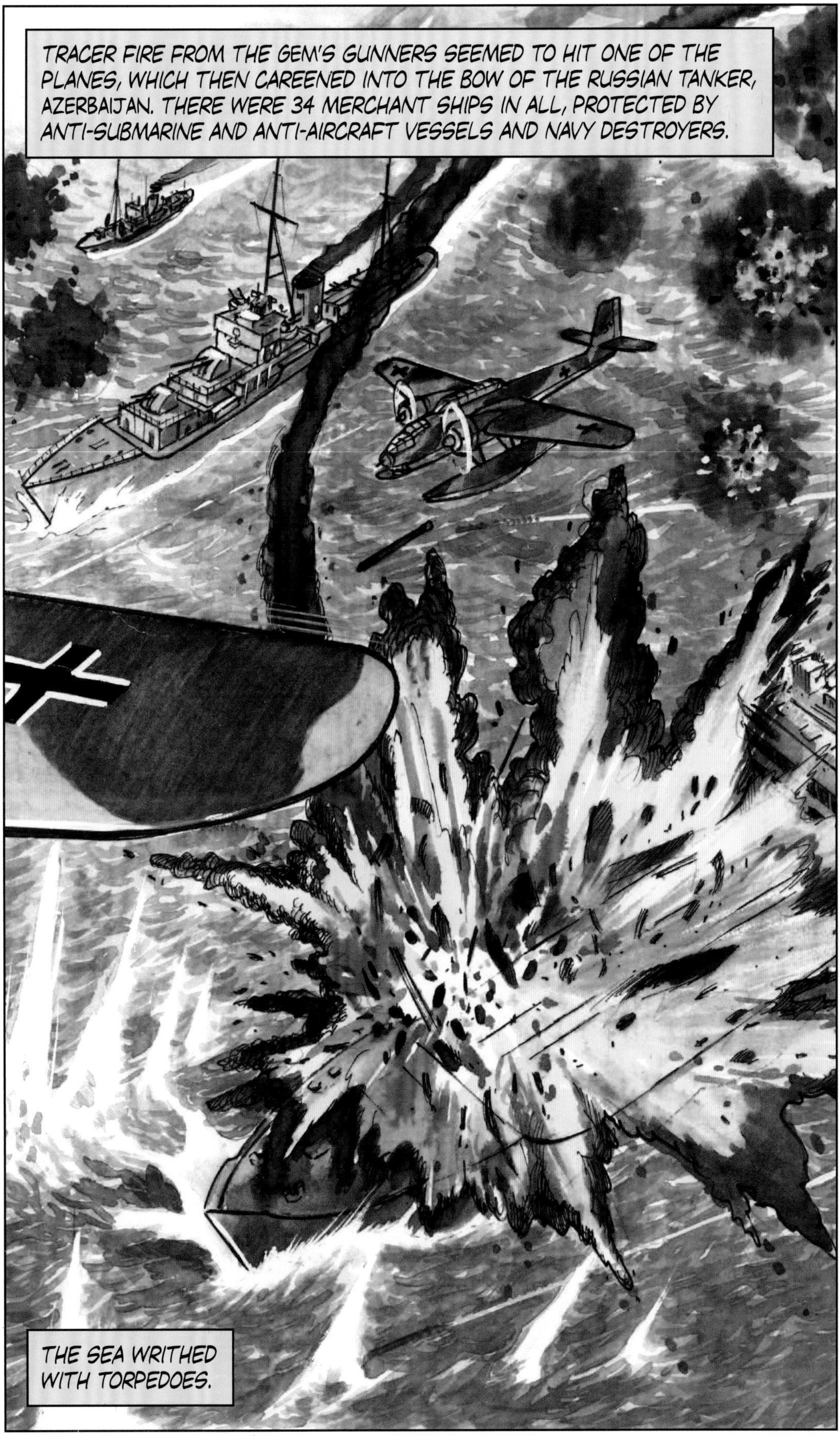
TRACER FIRE FROM THE GEM'S GUNNERS SEEMED TO HIT ONE OF THE PLANES, WHICH THEN CAREENED INTO THE BOW OF THE RUSSIAN TANKER, AZERBAIJAN. THERE WERE 34 MERCHANT SHIPS IN ALL, PROTECTED BY ANTI-SUBMARINE AND ANTI-AIRCRAFT VESSELS AND NAVY DESTROYERS.
THE SEA WRITHED WITH TORPEDOES.

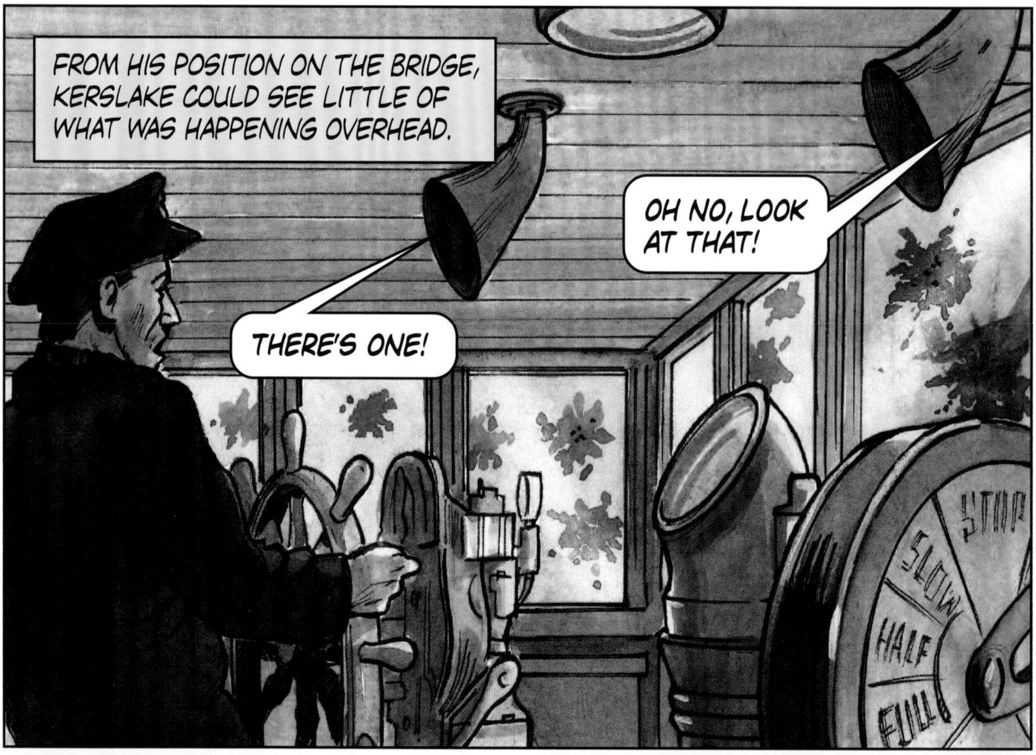
FROM HIS POSITION ON THE BRIDGE, KERSLAKE COULD SEE LITTLE OF WHAT WAS HAPPENING OVERHEAD.
OH NO, LOOK AT THAT!
THERE'S ONE!
STOP
SLOW
HALF
FULL

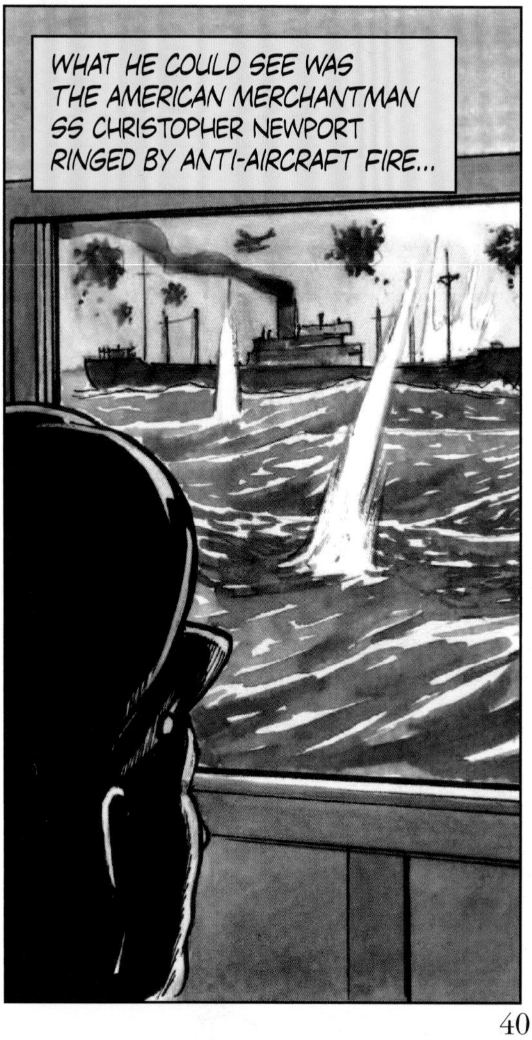
WHAT HE COULD SEE WAS THE AMERICAN MERCHANTMAN SS CHRISTOPHER NEWPORT RINGED BY ANTI-AIRCRAFT FIRE...

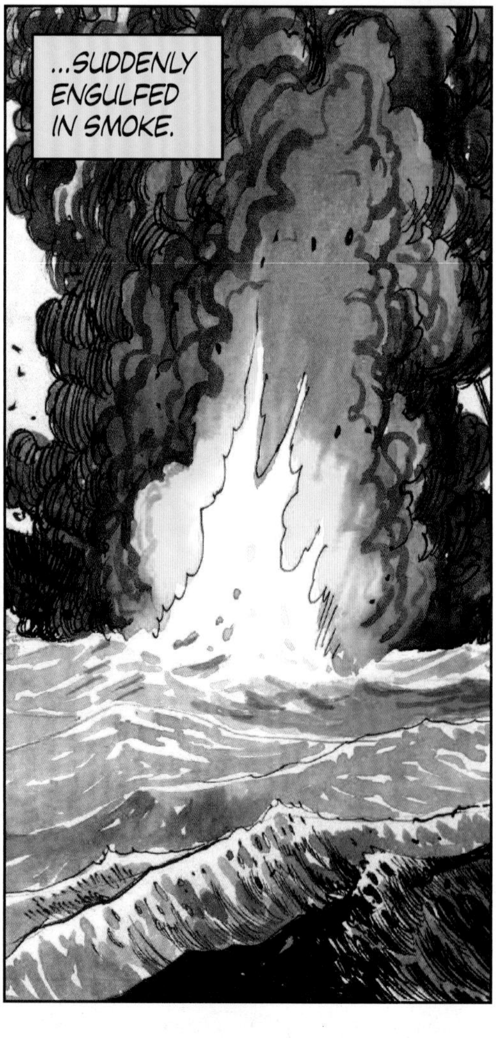
...SUDDENLY ENGULFED IN SMOKE.

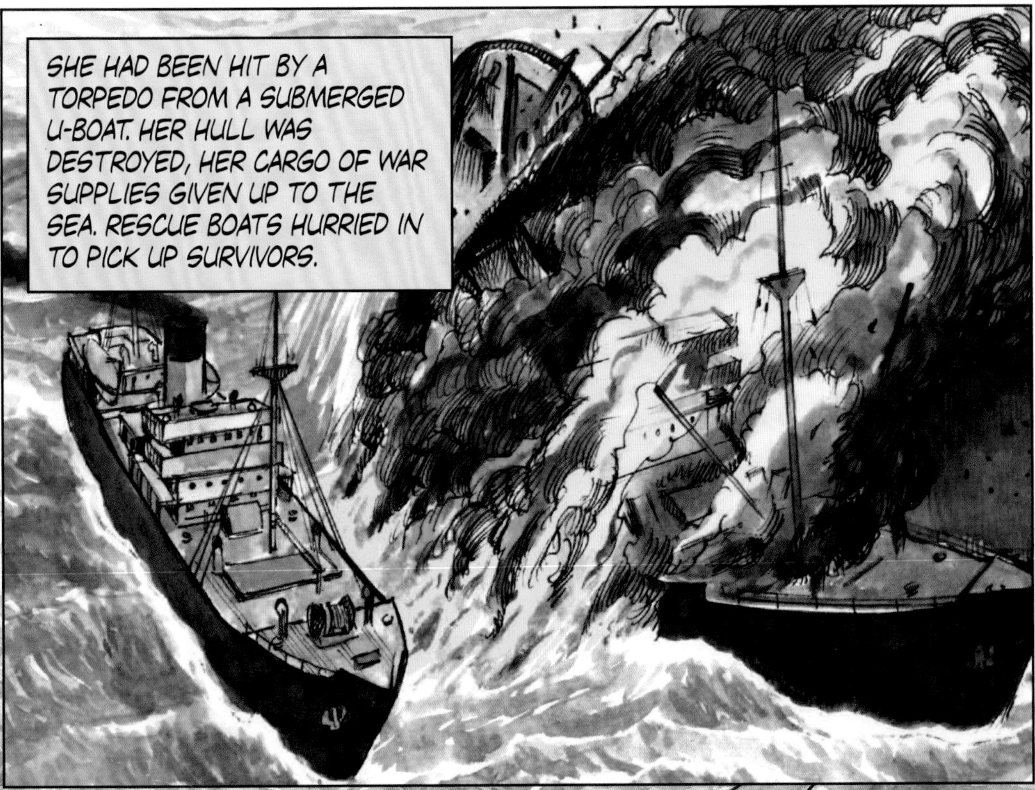
SHE HAD BEEN HIT BY A TORPEDO FROM A SUBMERGED U-BOAT. HER HULL WAS DESTROYED, HER CARGO OF WAR SUPPLIES GIVEN UP TO THE SEA. RESCUE BOATS HURRIED IN TO PICK UP SURVIVORS.

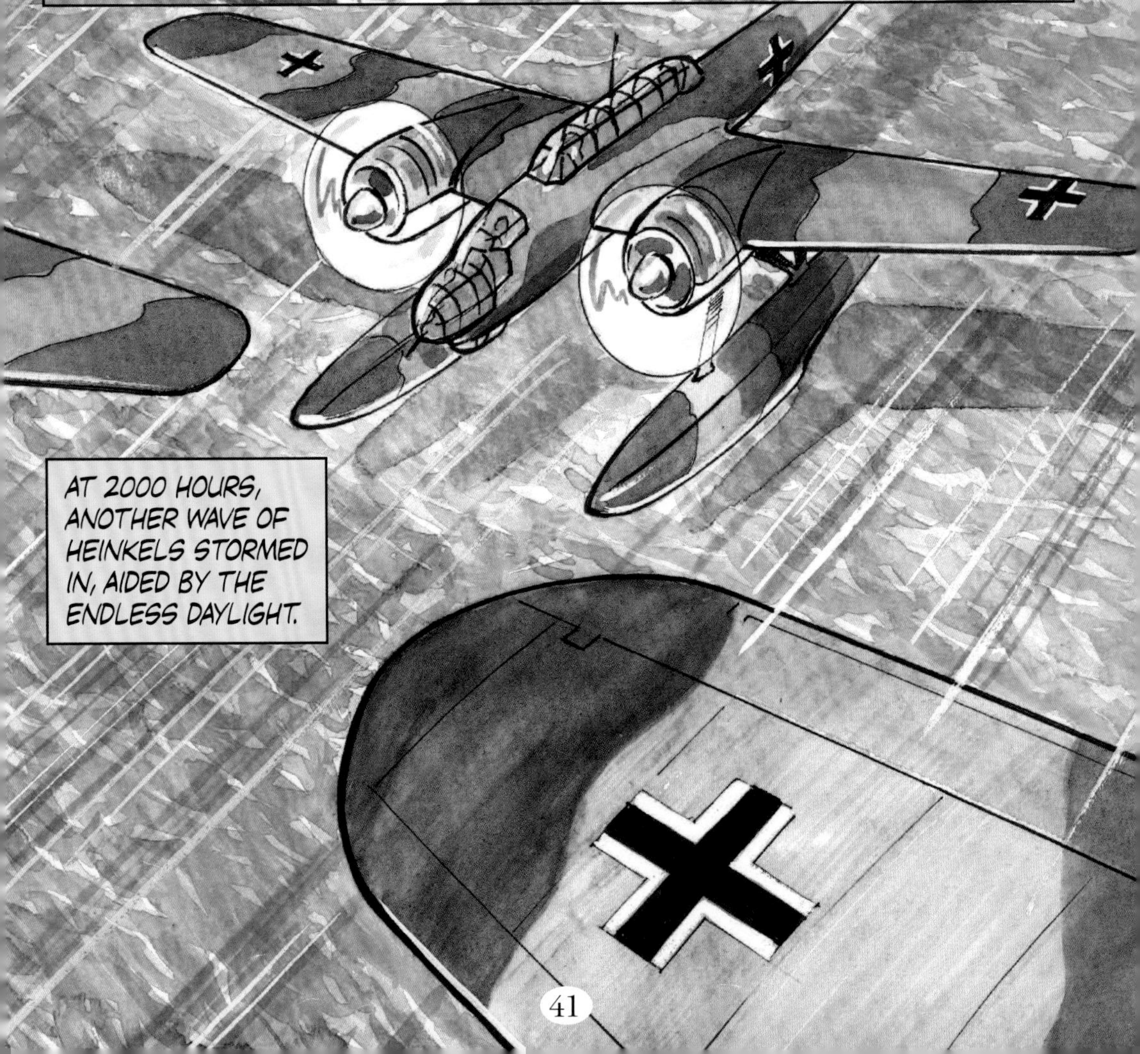
AT 2000 HOURS, ANOTHER WAVE OF HEINKELS STORMED IN, AIDED BY THE ENDLESS DAYLIGHT.

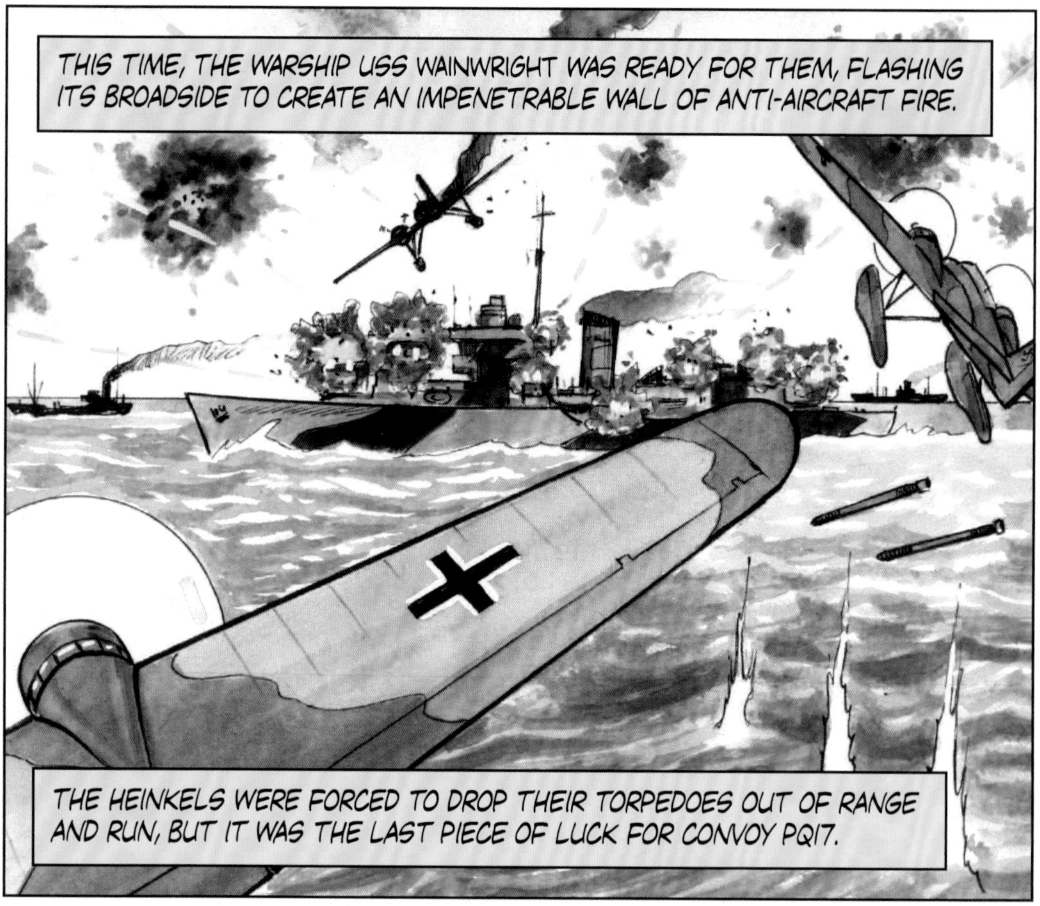
THIS TIME, THE WARSHIP USS WAINWRIGHT WAS READY FOR THEM, FLASHING ITS BROADSIDE TO CREATE AN IMPENETRABLE WALL OF ANTI-AIRCRAFT FIRE.
THE HEINKELS WERE FORCED TO DROP THEIR TORPEDOES OUT OF RANGE AND RUN, BUT IT WAS THE LAST PIECE OF LUCK FOR CONVOY PQ17.

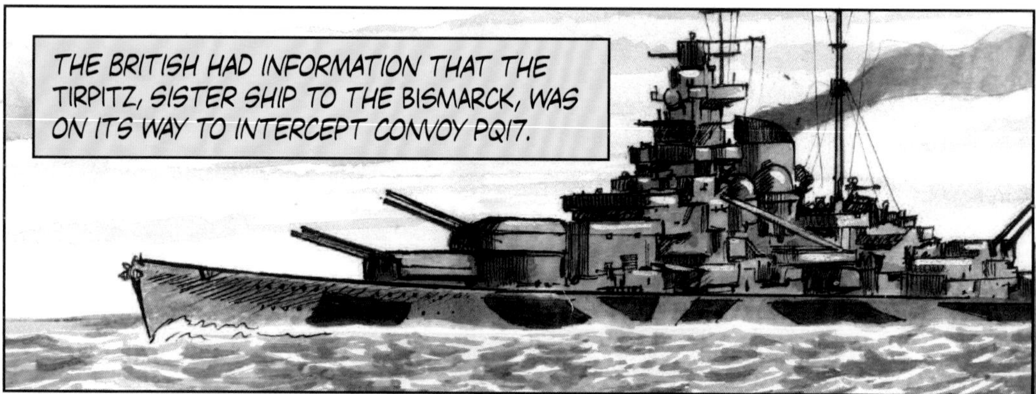
THE BRITISH HAD INFORMATION THAT THE TIRPITZ, SISTER SHIP TO THE BISMARCK, WAS ON ITS WAY TO INTERCEPT CONVOY PQ17.

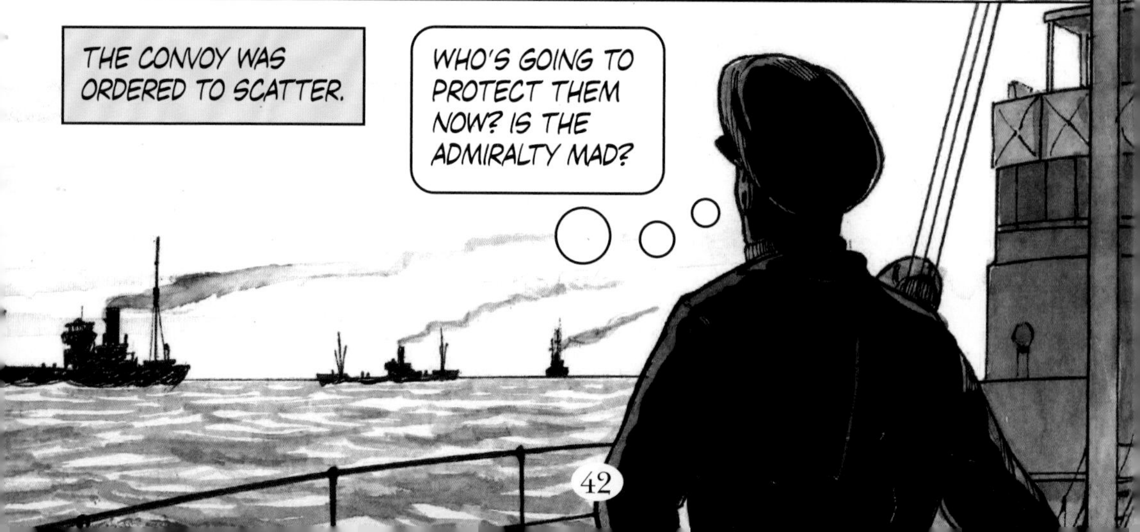
THE CONVOY WAS ORDERED TO SCATTER.
WHO'S GOING TO PROTECT THEM NOW? IS THE ADMIRALTY MAD?

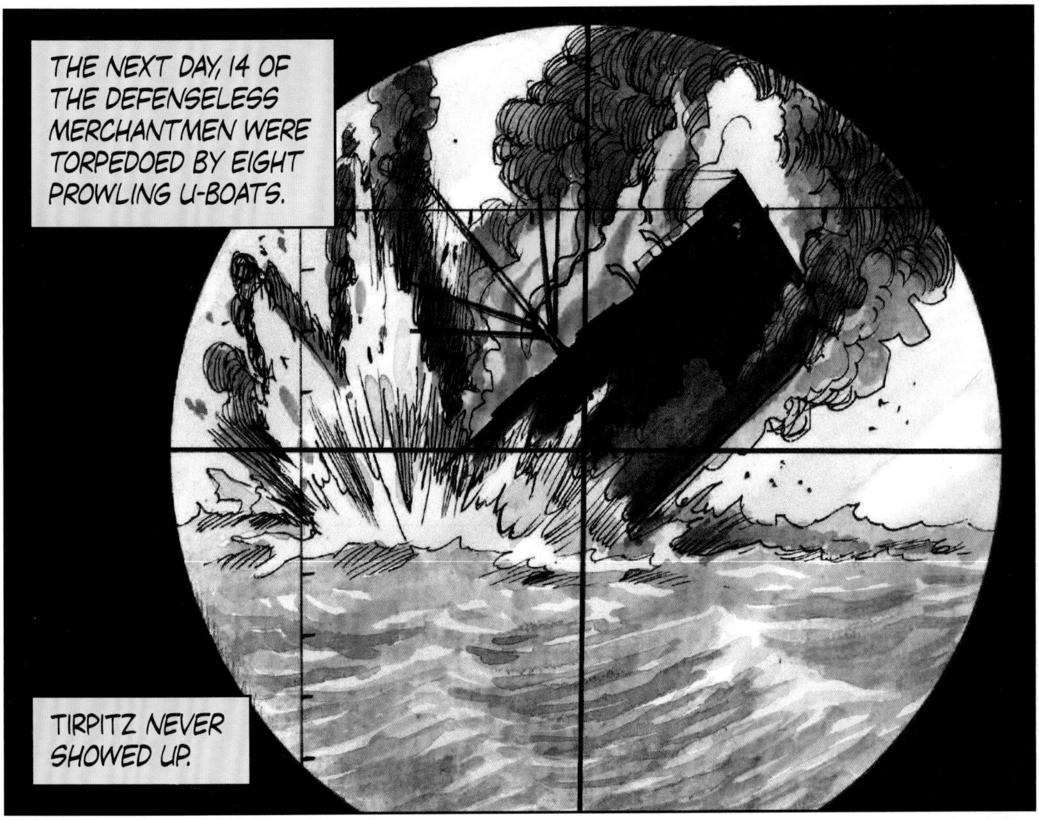
THE NEXT DAY, 14 OF THE DEFENSELESS MERCHANTMEN WERE TORPEDOED BY EIGHT PROWLING U-BOATS.
TIRPITZ NEVER SHOWED UP.

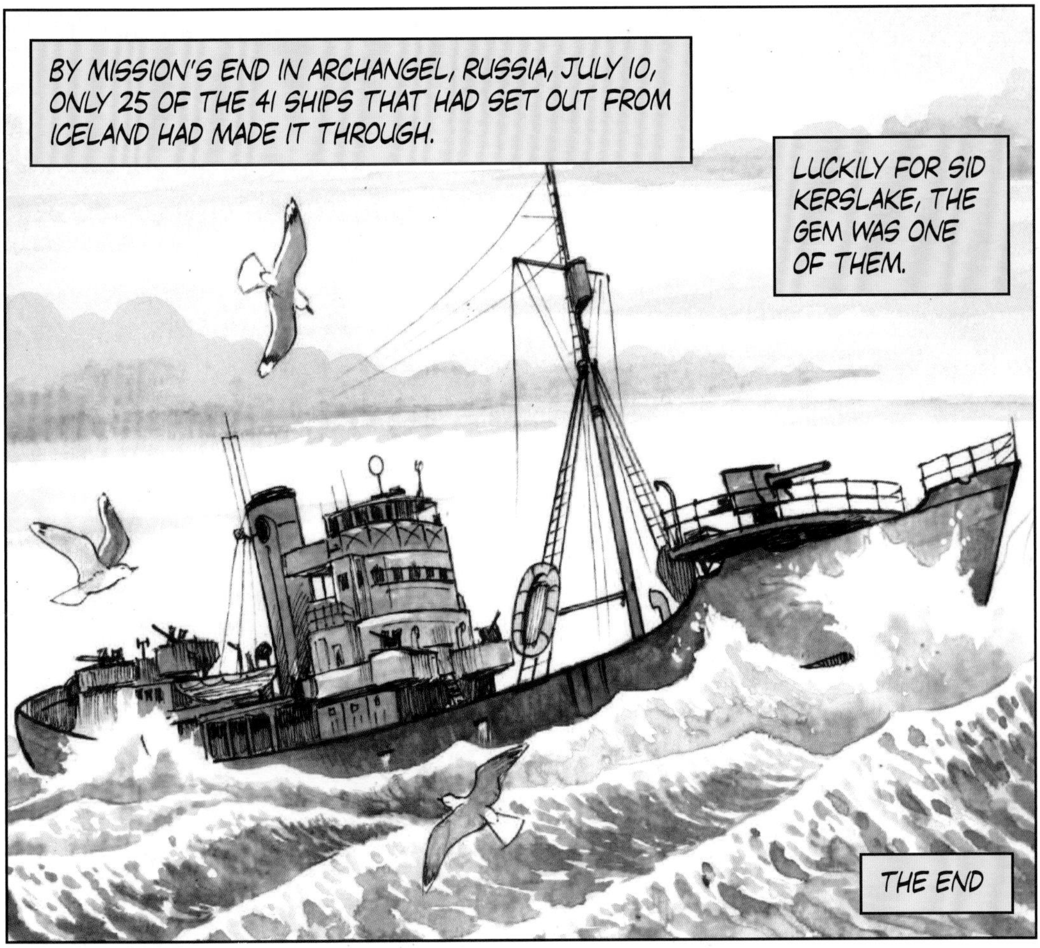
BY MISSION'S END IN ARCHANGEL, RUSSIA, JULY 10, ONLY 25 OF THE 41 SHIPS THAT HAD SET OUT FROM ICELAND HAD MADE IT THROUGH.
LUCKILY FOR SID KERSLAKE, THE GEM WAS ONE OF THEM.
THE END

FREEDOM OF THE SEAS

The first three months of 1942 had seen the sinking of 533 merchant ships off the coast of North America—a third of them were oil tankers bound for Britain. The US Navy was finally compelled to start a protected convoy system and, on April 14 claimed their first U-boat kill.

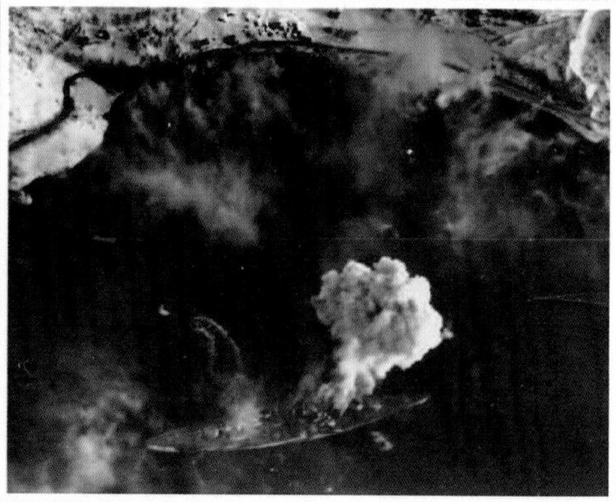

Tirpitz *was eventually sunk by British bombers in November 1944. Lack of fuel oil had kept her mainly in port since PQ17, allowing many future Arctic convoys to get through unscathed.*

ANALYSIS

To the British, it seemed too little too late. The Royal Navy and Merchant Marines were getting their tactics down to a fine art in the North Atlantic, with bigger and better protected convoys, but their analysis of the campaign to come disturbed them.

They calculated that if up to 25 new U-boats were being built every month, then by the end of 1942, Dönitz's fleet would number 400 subs. What the British didn't know was that Germans had also cracked the Royal Navy code, allowing U-boat controllers to pinpoint where convoys would be in the vastness of the Atlantic with perfect accuracy. The race to destroy Allied tonnage faster than it could be replaced was reaching its decisive moment.

IN THE "BLACK PIT"

From June 1942, Dönitz assembled the largest group of wolf packs so far. They were positioned in an area south of Greenland, the point where Allied aircover ended—the so called "Black Pit."

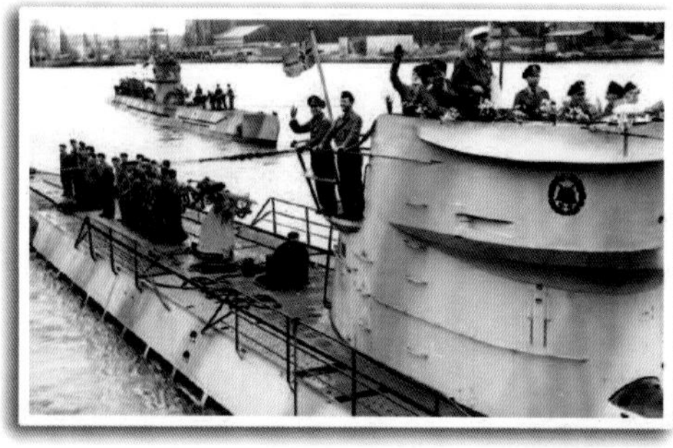

A U-boat crew returns victorious from the North Atlantic.

Aided by Allied signal intelligence, more than 200 operational U-boats sent down 904,684 tons (807,716 metric tons) of shipping in November alone. By year's end, the total would be 1,323 ships lost for 87 U-boats destroyed—an Allied disaster. Fuel stocks had dropped to a low point—Britain was literally running out of gas.

Crisis Point

Disastrous as 1942 had been, there was some light. On December 31, in the Battle of the Barents Sea, two German heavy cruisers had been beaten off by smaller British destroyers. Hitler was so angry, he threatened to scrap the entire surface fleet but accepted Admiral Raeder's resignation instead.

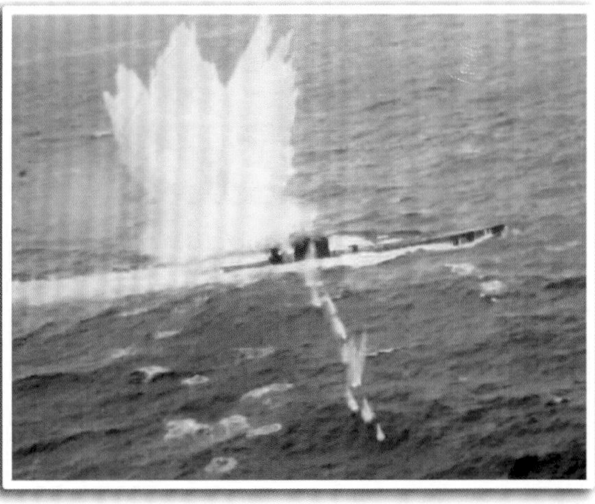

U-848 under attack by a B-25 Liberator in the South Atlantic. Attacks by long-range aircraft became a real hazard for U-boats in 1943.

Dönitz became supreme commander of the Kriegsmarine, but his joy was brief. In the first six months of 1943, the Allies met the challenge of the U-boats.

They equipped bombers with air-to-surface RADAR and put rangefinders on ships that could zero in on U-boat radio traffic. Missions were flown across the Bay of Biscay to attack U-boats traveling in and out of their French ports and, through tireless work, the codebreakers of ULTRA were once again able to read German signal traffic. At sea, the convoy escorts slowly scored more hits. U-boat losses became unacceptable and, on May 24, Dönitz halted the campaign and recalled the wolf packs. The Battle of the Atlantic was effectively won.

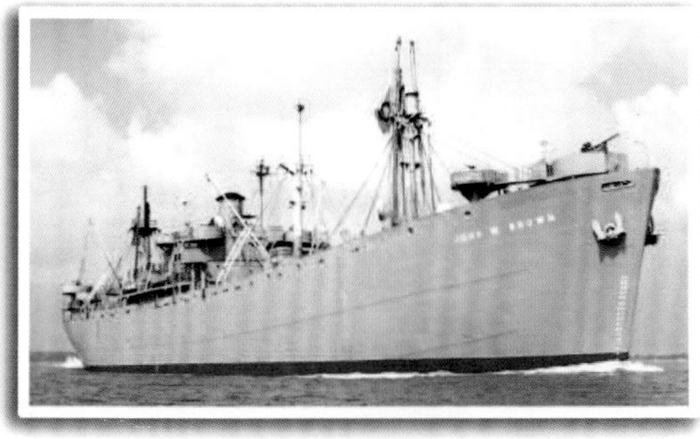

More than 2,700 Liberty ships were supplied by the USA to help replace those lost to the U-boats, ensuring the Allies won the tonnage war.

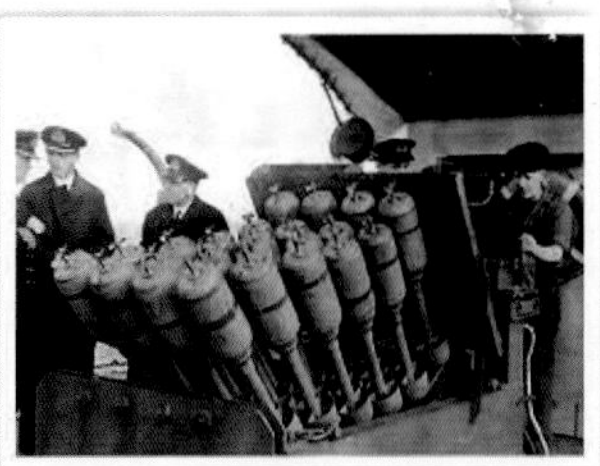

New anti-submarine weapons such as the Hedgehog multiple mortar thrower, were pioneered by the Allies.

Four Type XXI U-boats lie captured by Allied forces in Bergen, Norway, in 1945. With a specially designed battery, the XXI was intended to operate mainly submerged, unlike the previous U-boats that worked best on the surface.

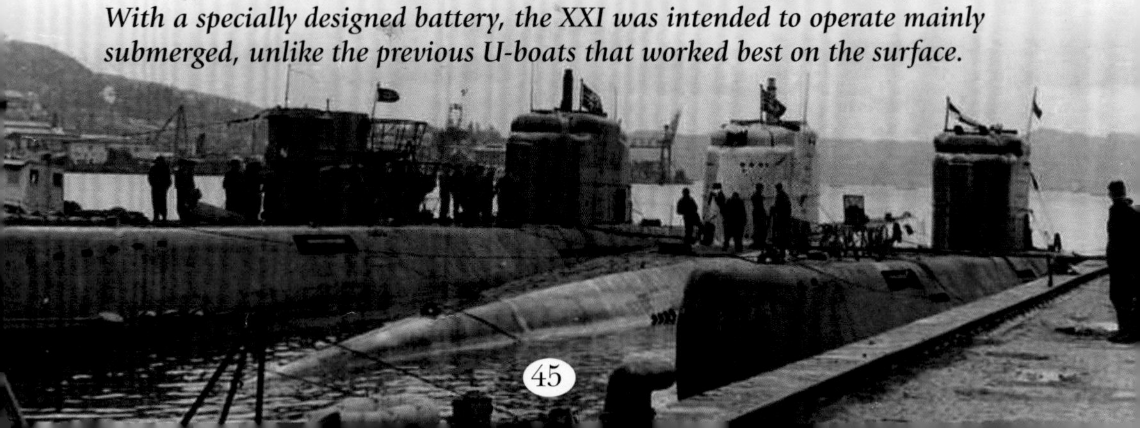

GLOSSARY

Allies The joint military forces fighting against Germany and Japan during World War II

Axis The joint military forces consisting of countries such as Germany and Japan that fought against the Allies during World War II

avenge To take revenge on behalf of someone or something

bow The front of a ship

broadside When all the guns on one side of a warship are fired

commerce The trading of goods between foreign countries

conning tower An observation point on a submarine

convoy A group of ships traveling together to increase their safety

depth charge A bomb used to sink submarines, and designed to explode at a certain depth

dilemma A difficult problem with no appealing solutions

Enigma The code machine used by Germany and its allies to send important messages during the war

escort A protective group of armed ships

hull The frame of the bottom of a ship

knot A unit of speed used by ships

mess The area of a ship where its crew eats and relaxes

neutral To refuse to support one side over another in a dispute

pandemonium A state of chaos

Life aboard a U-boat during the "happy time" in 1941.

periscope A device that uses mirrors to provide a view of an object that is above or below direct sight

port The left side of a ship

radar A device used to determine the presence and location of another ship or plane

resignation To voluntarily give up one's employment

salvo The simultaneous discharge of two or more military guns, bombs, or rockets

scuttle To sink or try to sink a ship by making holes through the bottom of the hull

sonar A device used to determine the presence and location of objects underwater

squadron A unit in the air force consisting of two or more flights

suicide To take one's own life

swell Movement of the waves on the surface of the sea

Swordfish A bomber plane that fires torpedoes

tonnage The amount of cargo a ship can carry

torpedo A form of explosive launched from a submarine and designed to explode on contact with another ship

tracers Chemical trails from ammunition that help shooters correct their aim

veteran One who has worked in a specific area for a long enough time to gain significant experience

A U-boat comes under heavy fire from US aircraft in 1943.

INDEX